ACTS for OUR TIME

CHARLES YRIGOYEN, JR.

ABINGDON PRESS / Nashville

ACTS FOR OUR TIME

Copyright © 1992 by Abingdon Press
Copyright © 1986 by Charles Yrigoyen, Jr.

This book is printed on recycled, acid-free paper.

Library of Congress Cataloging-in-Publication Data

YRIGOYEN, CHARLES, 1937-
Acts for our time / Charles Yrigoyen, Jr.
p. cm.—(Abingdon lay Bible studies)
Originally published: New York : General Board of Global
Ministries, United Methodist Church, 1987.
ISBN 0-687-00771-2
1. Bible. N.T. Acts—Criticism, interpretation, etc. I. Title. II.
Series.
[BS2625.2.Y75   1992
226.6'07—dc20   91-34035
                                                              CIP

Originally published in 1986 by the Women's Division of the General
Board of Global Ministries, The United Methodist Church.

The Scripture quotations in this publication, except where
specifically noted, are from the Revised Standard Version of the
Bible, Copyright 1946, 1952, © 1971 by the Division of Christian
Education, National Council of Churches of Christ in the U.S.A.
Used by permission.

MANUFACTURED IN THE UNITED STATES OF AMERICA

Preface

John Wesley reminded the "people called Methodist" that reading and studying the Bible is a means of grace. The scriptures are the primary place where we meet the living God, come to know God's will for us, and find the inspiration for our personal and corporate journey of faith.

It was with great joy that I accepted the invitation to write this study book on Acts. My intention throughout the following pages is to be faithful to the biblical text and to suggest some of the many places where it relates to what we think, say, and do. My task will have been achieved if I have helped the readers to begin to appreciate Acts as an exciting and profitable book, worthy of our careful reading and thoughtful contemplation. God calls us to have a 'faith in search of greater understanding' and a 'faith active in love.' Acts gives abundant illustration of many ways in which the earliest Christian community fulfilled this calling. God expects nothing less from us.

I wish to express my gratitude to those who have taught me to respect the scriptures and to look for God's word in them. They are too many to cite by name. I am especially grateful to my wife, Jean, who assisted me in preparing the manuscript and whose patience and encouragement is always more generous than I deserve.

—*Charles Yrigoyen, Jr.*

TO JEAN

whose life and love are the gift of God's grace

Table of Contents

CHAPTER I

Introduction to the Study of Acts

The Acts of the Apostles is one of the most fascinating books in the New Testament. It is also one of the longest. Some have called it the "history book" of the New Testament since it seems to be the story of the earliest years of the Christian community.

The episodes narrated in Acts were intended to present a picture of the early church as a dynamic community led by the Spirit of God, even as it was facing serious questions about its identity and mission. Similar issues confront the church in our time. A careful study of Acts, therefore, will not only help us to understand how the young church developed, but may also compel us to consider anew the nature of the church and its mission today.

Some Introductory Questions

What can be said about the traditional title of the book, the Acts of the Apostles?

Like other books in the New Testament, this one's title was most likely not assigned by its original author. In fact, as we will note later, Acts is the second half of a two-part document. If this larger work was given a title by its author, it appears to have been lost. The present title of Acts may have been given to it as late as A.D. 180 by a Christian writer named Irenaeus.

There are two interesting facts about the title of the book as we now have it. First, it is very doubtful that the author would have employed in the title the Greek term *praxeis* which is translated into English as "acts." While the word *praxeis* generally referred to a person's deeds or actions, it appears only once in Acts (19:18) and there it refers to wicked practices of magic that Christians should avoid. The writer would probably not want to confuse the readers of the book by giving it a title that was in any way associated with the pagan *praxeis* (acts) he advised them to shun.

Second, calling the book "The Acts of the Apostles" may be misleading. "Apostle" was a term used by Luke and in the early church to designate a special group of Jesus' disciples (Luke 16:13 and Acts 1:2). Apostles were thought to be specially commissioned by Jesus to be sent out in mission. Chief among them were the twelve* who are mentioned in Acts 1:13, 16 and Matthias, the successor to Judas (1:26). The only members of the twelve, however, who are mentioned by name after the first chapter of Acts are John, James and Peter. John is mentioned seven times and James only once. Peter is a major figure in the book, but does not appear after chapter 15. The author speaks about the "apostles" as a group several times throughout the book and refers to Barnabas and Paul as apostles (14:14). However, the author was as much interested in describing the deeds of other significant leaders who probably were not considered apostles in the early Christian community, such as Stephen, Philip, Priscilla and Silas. So, the acts of many of the most well-known apostles, particularly the twelve, are never described in the book while the acts of others not generally thought to be apostles, are prominently included.

Who wrote Acts?

It is usually agreed that the author of the Gospel of Luke was also the author of Acts. For that reason Acts is described as the second half of a larger work. These two books, the Gospel of Luke, and Acts, comprise about 25 percent of the New Testament. Some of the evidence for common authorship is as follows:

---

*Since only men could be legal witnesses in the first century, it is not surprising that "the twelve" were all men, though "apostle" (one sent) was also used at least no later than the third century in reference to Mary Magdalene as "an apostle to the apostles" (John 20:17–18), and the term "apostle" as one sent out on a mission was not restricted to men in the early church. (See Leonard Swidler, *Biblical Affirmations of Woman*, Westminster Press, 1979, pp. 209 ff.)

First, both books are addressed to "Theophilus." In the Gospel of Luke the author stated that he was writing "an orderly account" for the "most excellent Theophilus" so that he might know the truth about Jesus and his disciples (Luke 1:1–4). In Acts, his second book, also addressed to Theophilus (1:1), the author continued his narrative from Jesus' ascension to Paul's preaching in Rome, the capital of the empire.

Who was Theophilus? We are not sure of his identity. We know that the name was common in the ancient world and meant "lover of God." Some have suggested that Theophilus was a prominent individual since in the Gospel of Luke the author addressed him as "most excellent," a title which indicated great honor.

If Theophilus was the name of an actual individual, perhaps he was someone who needed more information about the Christian movement and who could use his influence to create a more favorable environment for it. Or, perhaps Theophilus was a patron of the author, someone already sympathetic to Christianity, who could aid the author in circulating his book. Others have proposed that Theophilus was not a specific individual, but any (and every) "lover of God" who would benefit from knowing more about God's witness in Jesus Christ and God's activity in the early Christian community. At any rate, common authorship of the Gospel of Luke and Acts is indicated by both books being addressed to Theophilus.

Second, there are resemblances between events and personalities in Luke and Acts. This is especially true when we compare the final sections of the two books where events in the life of Jesus correspond to events in the life of Paul to form an interesting comparative pattern. A few examples will illustrate. Both Jesus and Paul encountered vigorous opposition from the established religious leadership (Luke 22:54; Acts 24:1–8). Both were seized by a mob (Luke 22:54; Acts 21:30). Both were physically assaulted (Luke 22:63–64; Acts 23:2). In both cases a mob shouted for their execution (Luke 23:18; Acts 21:36). And in each account a centurion had a favorable impression of the main character (Luke 23:47; Acts 27:3). These and other similarities have led some students of the two books to conclude that the same author wrote both of them.

Third, from early times a number of Christian writers assumed that the Gospel of Luke and the book of Acts were written by the same person. Although the author did not specifically identify himself in either book, the name of Luke came to be associated with both. It was believed that this was the same Luke whose name appeared three times in the New Testament (Colossians 4:14; II Timothy 4:11; Philemon 24) and who was a physician, a close associate of the apostles, and a loyal companion of Paul. Recent scholarship has raised serious questions as to whether this Luke was the author of the Gospel that bears his name and the book of Acts so that many commentators prefer to say that while both books appear to have been written by the same person, we do not know the definite name of the writer. However, because Luke's name is associated with the Gospel of Luke, they are content to call "Luke" the author of both the Gospel and Acts. In what follows we have accepted the assumption that the author of Acts was also the writer of the third Gospel. We will call Luke the author of both.

When and where was Acts written?

It is very difficult to answer this question. Various proposals have been made. Some say that Acts was written as early as the sixties of the first century A.D. Some believe it was composed in the nineties or later. The seventies or eighties would be the approximate time for the writing of the Gospel of Luke to which Acts is related.

A number of suggestions have been made regarding the place where Acts was written. Antioch, Ephesus, Greece and Rome have been proposed, but we cannot be sure about any of these as the definite place of its origin.

The Purpose of Acts

Nothing is more important in beginning to study Acts than to determine why it was written. What purpose did the author have in mind when he composed his narrative?

Since Acts is the second volume of a two-part work, it is natural to view it as a continuation of the story the author had begun in the first volume. In the Gospel of Luke, the author described the witness and power of God in the birth, life, death and resurrection of Jesus. He ended the Gospel with a scene in which the risen Christ appeared to his disciples and "opened their minds to understand the scriptures" (Luke 24:45). Jesus said to them, "Thus it is written, that the Christ should suffer

4

and on the third day rise from the dead, and that repentance and forgiveness of sins should be preached in his name to all nations, beginning from Jerusalem. You are witnesses of these things. And behold, I send the promise of my Father upon you; but stay in the city, until you are clothed with power from on high" (Luke 24:46–49).

As Luke's Gospel ended with a commissioning and a promise of empowerment by God, Acts began with the same. The risen Christ said to his disciples, ". . . you shall receive power when the Holy Spirit has come upon you; and you shall be my witnesses in Jerusalem and in all Judea and Samaria and to the end of the earth" (Acts 1:8). In Acts we read about the fulfillment of this promise and the manner in which the disciples performed their mandate.

Acts, therefore, was intended to be an extension of the story begun in Luke's first book, his Gospel. It is a description of God's continuing witness and power in the earliest Christian community and the story of the community's faithful and courageous witness from Jerusalem to Rome.

Many faithful Christians for many centuries believed that Acts was an accurate historical record of the history of the early church. The reports of persons and events in Acts were accepted as fact since it was taken for granted that Luke had provided a reliable description of the apostolic age. Indeed, Acts does furnish us with a considerable amount of information about the first thirty years of the church's history that we would not have were it not for Luke's account.

Scholars, however, have raised serious questions about the reliability of the book as a trustworthy historical record, as we define "history" today. They have claimed that since Luke may not have had the necessary sources of information to write a correct history of the period, it is more reasonable to conclude that his major purpose was simply to present a positive portrait of the church as a community guided by the Spirit of God. For some of them, Acts is more like an historical reflection written by an early Christian theologian.

Those who have challenged the historical accuracy of Acts have pointed to some sections of the text that certainly raise serious questions about its dependability as an accurate historical record. For example, Gamaliel's speech to the council of the Sanhedrin (Acts 5:35–39) is an obvious case of confused facts. Gamaliel is reported by Luke to have cited two revolutionaries, Theudas and Judas the Galilean, in his speech. While in the Acts account Gamaliel said that Theudas' revolt took place before he delivered this speech, other reliable sources indicate that Theudas' activity occurred at least a decade after Gamaliel is said to have delivered his remarks. Furthermore, although Gamaliel in this account said that Judas the Galilean came after Theudas, there is evidence that the uprising led by Judas the Galilean happened decades before Theudas. Luke seems to have been confused about these facts.

In addition, scholars who have raised doubts about Luke's truthworthiness as an historian have also alleged that there are inconsistencies in the portrait of Paul in Acts and information about Paul derived from his letters. An illustration is Paul's first visit to Jerusalem after his transforming experience on the road to Damascus. In Paul's Jerusalem visit recorded in Acts 9:26–30, he is reported to have met with the apostles, told them about his encounter with the Lord, and described his bold preaching in Damascus. This does not seem to correlate with Paul's own account in Galatians 1:18–19 where he stated that when he visited Jerusalem after his conversion the only one of the twelve he saw was Peter (Cephas) along with James, the brother of Jesus.

Others have been quick to defend Luke as an historian of the early church. Recognizing that there are problems regarding some of the material in Acts, they have attempted to show that Luke was interested in much more than writing an historical account—he was interested in writing history with a purpose. They hold that he was well informed about the geography of the region. His knowledge about the political situation and the legal system of the period was accurate. The citation of approximately one hundred personal names shows his commitment to and fondness for historical detail. Furthermore, with regard to his portrayal of Paul there seem to be many points of agreement between Acts and Paul's letters. In such major matters as Paul's violent persecution of Christians before his Damascus road experience both Acts and the letters agree (see Acts 9:1–2; I Corinthians 15:9; Galatians 1:13). Even in matters of considerably less importance the two are in harmony. For example, the reports of Paul's being smuggled out of Damascus in a basket and let down over the city wall (Acts 9:23–25; II

Corinthians 11:32–33) are similar, though Paul in II Corinthians speaks of the Roman ruler who opposes him while Acts speaks of Paul's opponents as "the Jews."

Where did Luke secure the information he used in constructing his narrative? At least two sources have been suggested. First, the earlier chapters of Acts (1—15) appear to describe events in which the author did not personally participate. He may have gathered information for this section of the book from his contacts with persons who were participants in those events, such as Paul, Barnabas, Philip, and some of the apostles, or from other sources. The later chapters of the book (16—28) include events in which the writer himself may have taken an active role. In some of these chapters the writer made use of the pronoun "we," which may point to his personal involvement in the events (see 16:10–17; 20:5–16; 21:1–18; 27:1—28:16). Those who accept an early date for the authorship of Acts—i.e. between A.D. 70 and 80—suggest that other information used in the second half of Acts may have been provided to the author by Paul, or his acquaintances. Some, however, have suggested that Luke did not accompany Paul but had access to the diary of one of Paul's companions, which formed the basis for the "we" passages.

We may speak of Luke not only as an historian of early Christianity, but also a theologian who used and arranged his source materials for a specific purpose. He wanted to tell his story in a way that would make clear God's presence and power in the early church and depict the faithful and courageous witness of the early church to God's revelation in Christ. For this reason, some have referred to him as a "theologically-minded historian" and a "historically-minded theologian." William Neil observes,

> . . . Luke's Church history in Acts is no mere recital of what happened in these early decades; it is history written by a theologian and a preacher. Luke is convinced that God's redemption of the world and renewal of its life continues through . . . the Church. There is nothing casual or accidental in its growth and progress; . . . the Church advances irresistibly in the power of the Spirit. God's plan for the salvation of the world, which began through Israel and was crystallized in the life, death and Resurrection of Jesus, proceeds on its victorious way to its appointed end despite all obstacles and human perversity.[1]

Aside from its primary purpose of describing the history of the early church as a continuation of the story of God's presence and power in the life of the Jewish people, particularly in the life and ministry of Jesus, there may have been some secondary purposes. Luke may have been seeking to minimize the hostility of the Roman government during the last decades of the first century, particularly during the rule of the Roman emperors Nero (A.D. 54–68) and Domitian (A.D. 81–96). The failure of the governmental officials Sergius Paulus (Acts 13:7–12), Gallio (18:14–15), Felix (24:22–26) and Festus (25:24–27) to find Paul guilty of any crime and his respectful treatment at their hands is intended to show that any Romans who really knew what Christianity represented could find no fault in it deserving punishment. Whenever the officials did resort to hostile action against Christians, it was imposed because of pressure from other sources (12:2–3; 24:27). Much emphasis is placed in Acts on Paul's Roman citizenship (16:37–39; 22:25–29; 25:10–12) and his confidence that the Roman system of justice will prove his innocence (25:10–11). Furthermore, there appears to be an attempt throughout Acts to prove to the Romans that Christianity was legitimately related to Judaism and, therefore, was entitled to be treated with the tolerance that the government generally exhibited toward Judaism.

Still another purpose of the author was to remind his readers that God had a plan for the renewal of the whole human race. This divine plan to enrich human life began with God's election of Israel. It was to Israel that God's promises were originally given. The Jewish scriptures told the story of those promises and formed the basis upon which to understand the coming of the Messiah and the way of forgiveness and salvation that God initiated through him. Luke emphasized throughout Acts that Christianity was the continuation and fulfillment of Israel's religion. He was especially interested in showing the bonds that existed between the two. The church's earliest leaders were Jewish. Jerusalem, the holy city, was the first and most significant center of the church's life and thought. The temple remained an important place of prayer and testimony for Christians although its function as a place for ritual sacrifice was not stressed by Luke.

But Luke was also prepared to show how God was also

reaching out to the Samaritans and even to the Gentiles. Through the words and deeds of Philip, Stephen, Peter, Barnabas and Paul the message of God's plan of repentance, forgiveness, joy and new life through Christ received wider and wider circulation. No longer were women and men to think in narrowly racial, nationalistic or gender terms regarding salvation and new life. A new era had begun in which there was neither Jew nor Greek, slave nor free, male nor female. All were one in Christ Jesus (Galatians 3:28). Despite troubling controversy within the church and vehement opposition from the outside, Luke tried to show that it was God's intent to include every person in a new society—*all* could be blessed.

The Speeches in Acts

One of the prominent features of Acts is the collection of speeches made by various characters throughout the book. Some of them are quite long. For example, Stephen's speech in Acts 7 comprises almost the whole chapter. Briefly, we must note the importance of these speeches, which constitute more than 20 percent of the book, and say something about their style and content. More detailed comment will be made later when we read the speeches more carefully.

It is generally agreed by scholars that the speeches in the book were largely the free composition of Luke, author of Acts. The style, content and structure of the speeches have caused scholars to conclude that the speeches are not verbatim accounts of what was actually spoken, although they may very well represent the basic substance of what was actually said and believed by the persons to whom they were ascribed.

What purpose do the speeches serve? The major speeches of the leaders of the early Christian community, such as Peter, Stephen, and Paul, contain some of the basic ideas and claims of the Christian movement. H. J. Cadbury, a widely recognized authority on Acts, has observed that the apostolic message in the speeches may be summarized as follows:

The preaching of repentance by Jesus . . . though interrupted by the Crucifixion,˙was vindicated by God's raising him from the dead. This Resurrection points . . . to the future judgment for which Jesus is to return. Therefore, bearing witness to the Resurrection involves warning and a continued call to repentance . . . . God has overruled the stubbornness of [the human race], but will not sanction further disobedience.

The Jesus whom the disciples preach was designated by God as Lord and Christ (Messiah), or the prophet whose coming Moses and the prophets predicted. The Holy Spirit, who marks the experience of his messengers, also was anticipated. . . . But the evidence of the past and of the present throughout all the speaking in Acts is overshadowed by its futuristic appeal and warning. What their hearers may think about the past is of less importance than what it leads them to do now.[2]

Some Key Themes in Acts

It may be helpful to point out a few key themes in Acts even before we begin to examine more extensively various sections of the book.

First, throughout Acts it is really God who is the chief actor. This book may have been aptly titled the "Acts of God" as much as the "Acts of the Apostles." God's activity is mostly described as the work of the Holy Spirit, which is viewed by Luke as God's powerful presence active in human affairs. The Holy Spirit is mentioned fifty-seven times in the book.

Acts begins with a promise of empowerment for Jesus' followers through the Holy Spirit. The fulfillment of this promise would enable them to carry on their witness in Jerusalem, Judea, Samaria and to the end of the earth. Their mission could not be successful without the presence and energizing force of the Holy Spirit. Acts 2 contains the story of the gift of the Holy Spirit on the day of Pentecost. Thereafter, the Spirit, sometimes in extraordinary events and at other times in less spectacular ways, is the divine presence that changes human lives and builds the Christian community.

Moved by the Spirit, the early Christians preached the good news of God's forgiveness and new life available through Jesus. The Spirit supplied the inspiration and courage that made Christians speak and act boldly in the midst of dangerous and threatening circumstances. On some occasions the Spirit prodded the disciples to move into new territory where the gospel was needed. At other times the disciples were restrained by the Spirit from actions that were unwise. The Spirit attracted new believers, enabled the apostles and other leaders to work miracles, and provided insight to discern the forces of evil that sought to hinder God's work. Everything right that happened in the early church was understood by Luke to have been inspired, controlled and directed by the Holy Spirit.

It is important to note that the Holy Spirit was given to the early Christians in different ways. It was usually conferred through baptism. But there were times when baptism and the gift of the Spirit were not concurrent. In one incident, for example, Samaritan converts were baptized without receiving the Holy Spirit, which was later imparted to them through the "laying on of hands" (8:14–17). At another place believers received the Spirit before they were baptized (10:44–48). There was no uniform pattern of how and when the Spirit was given. Furthermore, it is important to point out that sometimes in Acts the reception of the Spirit by believers resulted in an ecstatically joyful experience such as speaking a divinely inspired language (10:46; 19:6). There are other times, however, where no such occurrence took place in connection with receiving the Spirit (8:17; 9:17–18).

Second, Acts offers a description of the life and worship of the early Christian community. From the brief summaries in its earlier chapters (for example, 2:42–47 and 4:32–35) we have a picture of the community's commitment to learning, fellowship, prayer, breaking bread, attending the temple and sharing possessions. Entrance into the community was by repentance, faith in Christ, and baptism with water. Its members were called "believers," "disciples," "saints," "brethren" members of "the Way," and "Christians." (The term "brethren" could be construed to include both men and women—brothers and sisters.)

The leadership of the community is depicted in only the briefest fashion. Jerusalem is identified as the early center of the church, the apostles as its principal leaders. They were assisted by elders who appear to be the heads of smaller local groups of Christians. Elders were charged with supervising the worship, instruction, discipline and administration of these units. There were also prophets and teachers in the primitive Christian community. The function of prophets was to admonish, console and encourage believers. Teachers were expected to inform the community with their clearer understanding of the faith.

Among the many leaders of the community mentioned by name in Acts, a few are singled out as outstanding and exemplary persons. One of them, of course, is Peter. Tradition clearly claims him as the preeminent head of the church in its earliest period. His sermon on the day of Pentecost, the healing miracles performed by his hand, his harsh treatment by the authorities, the confrontations with Ananias and Sapphira and Simon the magician, his role in the conversion of the Gentile named Cornelius, and his speech at the Jerusalem Council legitimizing the place of Gentiles in the church attest to his importance in Luke's view as the church's chief apostolic leader.

Luke also understood James the brother of Jesus to be a key leader in the early community. Even though James was not one of the twelve, he appears to have been the presiding officer at the Jerusalem Council where his speech was crucial in urging the acceptance of the Gentiles into the full membership of the church and in setting the conditions for their participation in its life.

While Peter is the commanding leader of the church in the earlier chapters of Acts, the later chapters are dominated by Paul. Luke pictured him as the converted persecutor of Christians who became Christ's premier missionary. By God's grace, surviving countless difficulties and overcoming opposition both inside and outside the church, Paul managed to retain his deep appreciation for his Jewish heritage while claiming that God's plan included the salvation of both Jews and Gentiles. Paul's mission work took him to the centers of pagan thought and life—Ephesus, Athens and Rome.

In Acts, the church is a community of God, meant to include all people. It is intended to transcend the customary barriers of race and nationality. So in Acts its membership includes Jews, Samaritans, Syrians, Greeks, Romans, and others. In Christ there was neither Jew nor Greek. The church's ministry was not limited by economic class. The wealthy merchant Lydia, the poor exploited slave woman, the middle-class Philippian jailer, were all the recipients of the church's ministry. In Christ there was neither slave nor free. The church was composed of women as well as men who used their gifts and talents in the service of Christ. In Christ there was neither male nor female. There was to be no discrimination of any type in the church based on race, class, nationality or sex.

Recent scholarship has demonstrated that Luke was especially interested in the role of women with regard to Jesus' ministry and the life of the early church. Throughout Acts women are numbered among Jesus' followers and occupy important roles in the community.

Women were among those who prayed for God's power and direction in the "upper room" following Jesus' ascension (1:14). The message about Jesus was addressed to them (16:18) and they were counted among those who responded favorably to it and believed (5:14; 16:14–15; 17:4, 12, 34), although on one occasion women were described in partnership with men as resisting the gospel and its messengers (13:50). Women converts as well as men suffered under Saul's persecution (8:3; 9:1–2; 22:4–5).

As Leonard Swidler points out, "Women were not merely converts to Christianity in its earliest phase but also critical workers in the spread and administration of Christianity."[3] Women opened their homes for Christian meetings (12:12; 16:14–15, 40). They collaborated in the work of spreading the gospel (18:1–3; 18:18–19) and shared the gifts and tasks of teaching (18:24–26), discipleship (9:36), and prophesying, that is, speaking on behalf of God (2:14–18; 21:7–9). Women constituted the early Christian community together with men and made important contributions to its life.

The author of Acts did not present a portrait of the church that overlooked its imperfections and faults. His was not a "happy history." He mentioned the dishonesty of Ananias and Sapphira, the church's neglect of the poor widows in Jerusalem, the heated debate regarding the admission of Gentiles into the church at the Jerusalem Council, the quarrel between Paul and Barnabas concerning John Mark, and the suspicion of some of the disciples regarding the authenticity of Paul's conversion. Luke did not paint an idealistic image of the church, but one in which faith and fault, God's intention and human pride were mixed. Even so, it appears that Luke minimized the bitterness between Paul and the church's leaders in Jerusalem over the issue of requiring Gentile converts to keep some provisions of the Jewish law (compare 15:1–29 with II Corinthians 10—13 and Galatians 2).

Third, Acts presents an understanding of the mission of the

Christian community. It is simply to bear witness to God's act in Jesus the Christ, the Messiah. Through him the blessings of salvation, forgiveness, and the gift of the Holy Spirit are available to everyone who turns to God. All who heed God's call to repentance and receive forgiveness and the gift of the Holy Spirit are united to others in a fellowship to experience joy and spiritual power.

Questions and Suggestions

Each of the chapters in this study book ends with some suggestions and questions. These are certainly not exhaustive in their scope. A careful reading and study of Acts should provoke additional ones. These, however, may be useful "to prime the pump" for discussion and action.

1. This book is arranged in a fashion that encourages a study of Acts in six sessions. It may be done in five sessions if the introductory material in Chapter I of the study book can be combined with the material in Chapter II. Even in five or six sessions, however, large amounts of the biblical text must be read and contemplated if the study is to be more than superficial. Therefore, a longer period of study should not be discouraged if needed.

2. This study book is simply an instrument to assist individuals and groups as they read the Bible for themselves and share their insights with each other. Reading the study book by itself cannot be a substitute for wrestling directly with the text of Acts and related biblical material. It is suggested that each person involved in the study read through Acts before the study begins to become acquainted with its overall pattern and message. The readers will then be better prepared to examine closely and profitably the various sections of Acts dealt with in the individual chapters that follow. The Revised Standard Version of the Bible has been used as a basis for this book, but the use of other versions, particularly in group study, is highly recommended. Participants in the group should be invited to share the insights they discover by using various translations.

3. We live in the most blessed generation ever to study the Bible. We have more resources available to help us read and understand it than any previous age. Bible dictionaries and

wordbooks, atlases of the geography of the Bible, commentaries to assist in interpreting the biblical text, and a large number of translations are ready for our use. This is especially true with regard to the study of Acts. A few resources are listed in the back of this book.

Among recent work recovering the role of women in the early church are books by Elisabeth Schüssler Fiorenza, Elizabeth M. Tetlow and Leonard Swidler. See the section on Resources.

While we need to read Acts in light of the circumstances and issues of our time, we must remember that we are not the first people to study this immensely beneficial book. We will enrich our study by seeking out and utilizing the insight and wisdom of others whose views about Acts are found in the large number of resources that may be secured to help us.

4. It may be interesting to recall what you remember about Acts from any previous study of it. Perhaps you have read all or parts of it in a church school class, discussed it in another group, or used it for personal meditation. What do you recall about it? What stories from Acts do you remember? If you have been asked to read through Acts in preparation for the study, share how your most recent reading of it compares with any impressions of the book you had previously formed.

5. We have observed that Luke was probably not a historian in twentieth century terms. One illustration is the speech of Gamaliel where there are inaccuracies regarding Theudas and Judas the Galilean. Does Luke's lack of accuracy about such historical facts lessen the value of Acts for us? Why or why not?

6. Acts may help us not only to understand the nature and mission of the early church, but also to consider the nature and work of the church in our time. Write a brief definition of the church and a description of its mission in no more than three or four sentences. (Participants could keep these statements until the study of Acts has been completed when they might reread them and share with the rest of the group how Acts may or may not have moved them to change what they originally wrote.)

Or, perhaps the group could work on a corporate definition of the church and its mission. This could be placed on newsprint and held for the last session when it could be reexamined.

7. In preparation for the next session read Acts 1:1—2:47.

CHAPTER II

God's Power and the Formation of the Christian Community
ACTS 1:1—2:47

The first and second chapters of Acts form a bridge between Luke's first book, his Gospel, and his second book, Acts, which contains his description of the spread of Christianity from Jerusalem to Rome. These chapters are an introduction to Luke's understanding of the nature and mission of the church. They cover the period from Jesus' ascension into heaven through Pentecost. The ascension and Pentecost events are still commemorated in the calendar of the Christian church. Jesus' ascension is observed annually on the fortieth day after Easter and is simply called Ascension Day. Pentecost is celebrated ten days later on the fiftieth day after Easter.

The Ascension of Jesus (1:1–14)

Acts opens with a reference to Luke's Gospel, his "first book," and an address to Theophilus whose identity, we noted earlier, remains a mystery. The author states that in his "first book" he told the story of what Jesus had said and done until the time of his ascension into heaven. In the last verses of the Gospel (Luke 24:46–53) he reported the risen Christ's final words to his followers. Jesus told them that they were his witnesses and that they were promised divine power, which would enable them to preach repentance and forgiveness to all nations. Before departing from them into heaven, Jesus gave them his blessing.

They joyfully returned to Jerusalem and constantly attended the temple praising God.

The earliest verses of Acts retell the last incident in the Gospel of Luke in more detail. In Acts 1:1–5 the author makes at least three important points.

(1) The fact of Jesus' resurrection is emphasized. Acts asserts that Jesus actually appeared to his followers for a period of forty days following his being raised from the dead. During this period they received instruction from Jesus that was to prepare them for their work as his witnesses. This is reminiscent of the divine instruction that Moses received for forty days at Mount Sinai (Exodus 24:12–18), which equipped him for his mission to the people of Israel and set forth God's plan for them.

(2) The central theme of Jesus' instruction was the kingdom of God, the complete rule of God on earth. According to Luke this was the principal theme of Jesus' preaching and teaching from the earliest days of his ministry (see Luke 4:43). Jesus spoke of the kingdom of God often, especially in his parables. His followers were taught to pray for its coming.

Many of Jesus' contemporaries also spoke about the kingdom of God, a concept that has roots in the Hebrew scriptures. The Old Testament notion of the kingdom, however, was frequently at odds with the rule of God that Jesus envisioned. For some, the kingdom was viewed in narrowly territorial and nationalistic ways. They believed that God's reign would encompass only their land, and that its benefits were reserved solely for the faithful of Judaism. Furthermore, some held that the kingdom would arrive only through a bloody militaristic revolt against the Romans who occupied and controlled the "holy land" given by God to the descendants of Abraham and Moses. On the other hand, Jesus taught that the kingdom of God was not limited to any specific geographical territory. It was present wherever God's will was accomplished. He also claimed that the kingdom was being initiated in his own ministry rather than by means of an insurrection against the Romans. Jesus stated, however, that the fullness of God's reign was yet to be realized.

The kingdom of God was to remain a central theme in the church's preaching and testimony (see Acts 19:8; 20:25; 28:23; 28:31).

(3) Before parting from his followers, Jesus told them that

they must not leave Jerusalem. (Compare Acts with Matthew 28:10 and Mark 16:7 where the disciples were directed to go to Galilee.) Luke emphasizes the point that they were to stay together and they were to wait for the fulfillment of God's promise of empowerment. Without empowerment their mission could not be successful. God had vowed to pour out the Holy Spirit on them bringing a new vitality and perserverance to their witness. They were to be "baptized with the Holy Spirit."

What was this Holy Spirit? It was the mysterious presence and power by which creation had taken place and by which the judges, kings and prophets of Israel had been inspired and invested with the gifts to accomplish their work. The Spirit represented God's presence in the covenant community of Israel. It was the same Spirit that had attended the life and ministry of Jesus. This same dynamic and energizing presence was promised to Jesus' followers.

Throughout Acts the Holy Spirit provides the motivation and direction for the ministry of the early Christian community. At the time Acts was written the church had not yet developed the theologically elaborate understanding of the Holy Spirit it would come to adopt later. As it did, the church viewed the Holy Spirit as something more than an impersonal power. It decided that the Spirit was nothing less than one of the three "persons" of God, the third person of the Trinity. The church relied on Acts as well as other biblical and theological sources in reaching this conclusion.

In the next section of the chapter (1:6–11) the disciples inquired of Jesus whether it was now time for God to "restore the kingdom of Israel." This would not be an unusual question. Jesus' earthly ministry had been concluded. God had raised him from the dead and he had appeared to his followers in order to teach them more about the kingdom. He had promised that God would soon fill them with the divine presence and power. It was quite natural for them to speculate about whether the complete rule of God was about to be achieved, even if they thought of it only in terms of the restoration of Israel. They wondered whether they were living in the last days before God's total rule would be consummated.

Jesus' answer was abrupt. It was not their business to know the time that God had fixed for the completion of the kingdom.

Preoccupation with such speculation was a diversion from the critical work that Jesus was commissioning them to do.

Despite Jesus' discouraging his disciples from engaging in speculation about the time when the kingdom would be completed, many Christians since those early days have yielded to such preoccupation. Some have been so bold, and so foolish, as to set dates for the fulfillment of the kingdom, which they have usually associated with the return of Christ and the "last days." In every generation since the first century some have believed that theirs was the era in which the kingdom would finally be perfected. William Miller, the famous Adventist leader of the nineteenth century, was absolutely convinced that Christ would return to earth and the kingdom would be completed sometime in 1843 or 1844. Regrettably, this type of theological exercise distracts Christians from the mission Jesus has committed to them. The kingdom will be completed in God's time, which is always the right time.

What were the disciples to do between Jesus' ascension and the completion of God's kingdom? They were to receive the power of the Holy Spirit and they were to be Jesus' witnesses. In their words and deeds they were to proclaim what they had seen and heard of God's justice, power and love in the life, death and resurrection of Jesus. And they were to take this mission, this witness, to an ever-widening audience—to Jerusalem, to all Judea, to Samaria, and "to the end of the earth." Thus, claims Luke, Jesus set the agenda and the itinerary for the early Christian community and for its successors.

After Jesus had finished his speech to the disciples, he ascended into heaven. He was lifted up and taken out of their sight on a cloud. Although some prefer to view this literally as it was pictured by Luke, others have suggested that it should be interpreted symbolically. For example, William Neil has said,

It would be a grave misunderstanding of Luke's mind and purpose to regard his account of the Ascension of Christ as other than symbolic and poetic. He is not describing an act of levitation, or bracketing the last event in the story of the historical Jesus with the legendary end of Elijah or Hercules. . . . In this case, the truth to be conveyed to the readers is that the end of the story of Jesus and the prelude to the story of the Church was the apostolic conviction that the risen Christ was now raised to the right hand of God, exalted as Lord and King.[1]

According to Luke, the disciples stood looking up into heaven as Jesus was lifted up on the cloud. Suddenly, two angelic beings, divine messengers, appeared and scolded them. Why were these disciples standing by idly and gazing into heaven? Jesus would return to them. But in the meantime there was a mission to accomplish. Jesus had told them what they were to be and what they were to do. They must not be distracted by a fascination with the place where they were standing or by a longing to flee from their earthly task on a heavenly cloud with their Lord. The disciples must be prepared to move on, ready to receive the gift of God's empowerment and the ministry for which Christ had chosen them.

The disciples traveled the short distance (less than a mile) from the Mount of Olives, where the ascension had taken place, to Jerusalem. They went to "the upper room." (It is unclear whether this is the same upper room where Jesus' last supper with his disciples occurred.) The author listed as present: Peter, John, James, Andrew, Philip, Thomas, Bartholomew, Matthew, James the son of Alphaeus, Simon the Zealot, and Judas the son of James. They were accompanied by a group of disciples who were women. Luke frequently mentioned the importance of women among the followers of Jesus (for example, Luke 8:1–3; 23:55–56; 24:10) and women continued to be significant disciples in Acts. Also present were Jesus' mother and his brothers. It is important to note here that in the upper room, unlike in the temple and the synagogues, men and women engaged in prayer together.

Luke's picture of the group in the upper room emphasized their unity and their prayerful waiting for the divine empowerment Jesus had promised. They knew that God would prepare them for the future that lay ahead.

A Replacement for Judas Iscariot (1:15–26)

The second half of the first chapter deals with choosing a successor to Judas Iscariot, the apostle who had betrayed Jesus. The early Christian community was convinced that Jesus' choosing *twelve* apostles was significant. That specific number corresponded to the twelve tribes of Israel. The followers of Jesus, later the church, regarded themselves as the new Israel. (See Luke 22:28–30.) To complete their number, they needed a twelfth person to fill the spot left vacant by Judas' desertion and death.

Peter is portrayed as the leading personality among the apostles in this section and makes the first lengthy speech in Acts. The text says that he delivered his words to about 120 persons. Why was Luke so precise regarding the number of those present? Perhaps the reason is that according to Jewish law 120 *men* were required "to establish a new community with its own council."[2] Luke was showing, therefore, that this infant Christian group (including both men and women) was a legitimate community that sought to meet the normal qualifications prescribed by the Jewish law.

Peter's address is the first of several important speeches ascribed to him in Acts. It contains at least two parts. In the first part (1:16–20), Peter speaks about the role of Judas in the arrest of Jesus, and Judas' death. Peter indicates that Judas' treachery had been foretold in scripture. Despite his having been a fully accepted member of the twelve apostles and a complete participant in their ministry with Jesus, Judas had acted as the chief accomplice for those who arrested and executed Jesus. Peter's speech offers a gory account of Judas' death. Peter claims that Judas had purchased a field with the money he was paid to betray Jesus. In that very field, Judas had fallen down and his body had burst apart causing his death. The people of Jerusalem, knowing what had happened to Judas, referred to his field by an Aramaic word, *akeldama*, which meant, "field of blood." Using two quotations from scripture (Psalm 69:25 and Psalm 109:8), Peter states that the desolation of Judas' field and the necessity of seeking a successor to the betrayer were foreseen centuries earlier. It was typical of the early Christians to relate personalities and events in their own time to texts in what we now call the Old Testament.

One of the main problems with the account of Judas' death in Acts is that it differs from the version given in the Gospel of Matthew. Matthew said that Judas returned to the religious leaders the money he had received for betraying Jesus. He then hanged himself. The chief priests used the "blood money" to purchase a field in which strangers were to be buried. This plot was called "the Field of Blood" because of the "blood money" with which it was bought (Matthew 27:3–10). While some have tried to harmonize the accounts in Matthew and Acts, they probably represent two different traditions of interpretation about Judas' fate.

The second part of Peter's speech (1:21–22) sets the basic qualification for the one who is to fill the vacancy among the twelve. It was to be someone who had accompanied the twelve throughout the ministry of Jesus from the time of his baptism by John through his recent ascension into heaven. An eyewitness to the events of Jesus' ministry could be trusted to know and speak the truth about his words and deeds. It was such a person that they sought to join the twelve in their work as witnesses to Jesus' resurrection.

In response to Peter's speech the names of two qualified men were submitted.* They were Joseph and Matthias. The community entered into prayer and asked for God's guidance in the selection of a successor to Judas. Furthermore, they "cast lots" to determine who should fill the vacant place. Casting or drawing lots was a common practice in ancient Israel and in New Testament times to discover the will of God. It was thought that this method of making a decision minimized any human element that might be involved. To cast lots in this case meant that the names of the candidates were probably inscribed on stones. The stones were then placed in a container and the container was shaken until one of the stones fell out. The one whose name was on that stone was considered chosen by God.

The "lot fell on Matthias." We know nothing about Matthias' background. He is not mentioned anywhere else in Acts or in any other book of the New Testament. Like others among the twelve, such as Bartholomew and Simon the Zealot, Matthias apparently occupied a quiet and somewhat obscure role. He was not an apostolic leader in the same manner as Peter, but presumably he participated fully in the ministry of the twelve, shared their authority, and was held in the same high esteem.

So, the disciples had received their instruction. They had been commissioned as Jesus' witnesses "to the end of the earth." Jesus had ascended into heaven. The apostolic leadership of the community was again at full strength with the enrollment of Matthias. It remained for the community to receive the promised empowerment by God.

*See footnote, p. 2.

The Day of Pentecost and the Gift of the Spirit (2:1–41)

The first chapter in Acts is really a prelude to the events described in the second chapter. The Holy Spirit promised in Acts 1 was given in the unusual circumstances narrated in Acts 2. The story is divided into three parts.

In the first part (2:1–13) we are told that the Spirit was conferred on the community on the day of Pentecost and was accompanied by extraordinary happenings. Pentecost, which means "fiftieth," was a religious observance that had its roots in the history of Israel. It was one of the most important annual festivals in the Jewish religious calendar. In the Old Testament, it is described as an agricultural festival that celebrates the wheat harvest (Exodus 23:14–17; Deuteronomy 16:9–12, 16). It was an occasion on which God's people were expected to show their gratitude for the first fruits of the harvest. Its common name was the Feast of Weeks. This festival was also associated with the occasions on which God made a covenant with Noah and later gave the law to Moses on Mount Sinai. Perhaps the Christian Pentecost was meant to be understood as the counterpart to the events at Sinai. Just as the Feast of Weeks commemorated the gift of the old covenant law, fifty days after Passover, so Pentecost marked the gift of the new covenant Spirit given on the fiftieth day after Easter.

Luke emphasized that the Pentecost event involved the hearing, seeing and feeling of those who participated in it. On several occasions in his Gospel and Acts he described extraordinary sights and sounds accompanying the presence of the divine in human affairs (Luke 3:21–22; 9:30–31; Acts 9:3–6; 10:10–15; 18:9–10).

When the disciples were all together in Jerusalem on the day of Pentecost, Luke stated that there was a sudden sound from heaven like a rushing wind followed by tongues of fire, which appeared to be resting over each of them. These were signs that God was breaking into human affairs in a marvelous and remarkable manner. Wind was a biblical symbol for the creating and renewing power of the divine Spirit (I Kings 19:11; Ezekiel 37:9; John 3:8) and fire was a symbol of God's holy and forceful presence (Exodus 3:2; Exodus 19:18).

Luke reported that the disciples were filled with the Holy Spirit and began to speak other languages under the inspiration of the Spirit. Being filled with the Spirit here means that these persons experienced the outpouring of the Spirit in their total beings. The significance of speaking in other tongues is explained in the verses that follow (2:5–13). Since Pentecost was one of the major festivals of the Jewish religious calendar, many faithful people from diverse places traveled to Jerusalem to celebrate the feast. Furthermore, in Judaism, pious persons from all over the world hoped to spend the final days of their lives either in or near Jerusalem. On the day of Pentecost, therefore, there were devout people in Jerusalem from many different nations and cultures. They represented a wide diversity of languages. Yet they heard the disciples of Jesus proclaiming God's deeds in their own native languages. How could this be since the disciples were simply common Galileans who had no knowledge of the languages of other lands? Luke registered dismay among the listeners. Some asked what all of this meant. Others dismissed the incident by accusing the disciples of being drunk.

It should be noted that for Luke, the speaking in tongues on Pentecost appears to differ from the speaking in tongues mentioned in 10:46 and 19:6. On Pentecost it referred to the gospel's being preached in *known* languages, familiar to the listeners. For this reason it has been suggested that Pentecost represented the reverse of the confusion of languages in the Tower of Babel story (Genesis 11:1–9). In the later chapters of Acts the "tongues" appear to be an unknown language uttered under the inspiration of the Spirit.

What was the meaning of the Pentecost event? There seems to be little doubt about what Luke intended to convey in these verses. The disciples were invested with the power they needed to fulfill Jesus' commission. They experienced the presence of God in a dynamic and transforming way. Their speaking diverse languages not only anticipated the universal mission of the church, but also indicated that in Christianity there could never be a supremacy of one tongue or culture over any other.

The second part of the chapter (2:14–36) consists of Peter's address to the assembled crowd. Luke presented it as a summary of what Peter said and as the first sample of Christian preaching. Peter, who stood among the other eleven apostles, was clearly their representative as he delivered his speech. He had been remarkably transformed by the Spirit from the timid

24

and fearful person who had renounced Jesus (Luke 22:54–62) to one who boldly and confidently proclaimed the good news of God's acts in the life, death and resurrection of Jesus.

Following his opening remarks to the crowd, Peter answered the charge of the skeptics that the disciples were merely drunk. Since it was only the third hour of the day (nine o'clock in the morning), it was not possible for them to be filled with new wine. Instead, what the crowd had witnessed was the outpouring of God's Spirit, foretold by the prophet Joel (Joel 2:28–32). The Old Testament prophet had predicted that the Spirit would be given to all, to women and men, to young and old, to slave and free. Wonders and signs would attend the Spirit's presence. Luke spoke of "wonders and signs" in Acts no less than nine times between 2:19 and 15:12, underscoring the mysterious and marvelous acts accompanying the Spirit's presence. What God had promised, therefore, had been realized in the life of Jesus' disciples and was available to any and all who called on God for their salvation.

Peter focused his remarks on Jesus, the one whose ministry had been attested by God with great works, wonders and signs. Jesus had been crucified by lawless and defiant people. But his death was neither an accident nor a disaster. It took place according to the plan of God. Death could not hold Jesus. God raised him from the dead just as the author of Psalm 16:8–11 had foreseen (compare Acts 2:25–28). The disciples were witnesses to the risen Jesus who had ascended into heaven as the exalted one of God. The same Jesus who had been brutally crucified had become what God had intended him to be, Lord and Christ. He had poured out the Spirit on his followers, the results of which the crowd was observing.

The third part of the chapter (2:37–41) provides a record of the response of the crowd. Moved by Peter's testimony, the people asked him and the other apostles what they should do in light of what they had heard. Peter's response was threefold.

(1) Repentance was required. This involved more than being sorrowful for one's sin. It meant *turning away* from everything that displeased God and robbed one of the fuller life God intended all to have. It also implied a *turning toward* God whose will was to lead persons to a more abundant life.

(2) Those who repent should also be baptized in the name of

Jesus to receive forgiveness of their sins. Baptism was not something totally new. For Gentiles who wished to become Jews, baptism (or a ritual bath) was common, as was circumcision for male Gentiles. Baptism was a sign of initiation into the people of God. In the early Christian community it was a means by which God's grace, God's unmerited love, entered a person's life. It was a symbol of divine forgiveness and cleansing. And it was a way of incorporating the person into the community of the Messiah, the Christ.

(3) Following repentance and baptism, the person would receive the gift of the Holy Spirit, the transforming presence and power of God, which Peter's audience had already witnessed in the events preceding his address. The promise of forgiveness and empowerment was for everyone, Peter asserted. It was for those present, their descendants, and all who were far off.

Luke's speech ended with Peter's exhortation to his listeners that they should flee from the wicked and corrupt generation in which they lived, a generation that had not only ignored God's anointed one (Messiah), but had killed him.

According to Luke, Peter's sermon achieved astounding results. On that very day about three thousand people became followers of Jesus and were baptized. Furthermore, there was no record of scoffing or opposition. That would appear later as the disciples extended their ministry and proclamation to other places.

The Life of the Early Christian Community (2:42–47)

In the closing verses of the second chapter, Luke provided a brief sketch of the life of the early Christian community in Jerusalem.

First, he outlined the manner in which the new converts were nurtured. They were steadfastly devoted to what some have called the four foundations of the early church. These were: (1) the teaching of the apostles; (2) fellowship; (3) the breaking of bread; and (4) prayer. We need to say something about each of these.

If anyone knew what Jesus had actually said and done, it was the twelve who were eyewitnesses to his ministry and resurrection. They were the guardians of the truth about him.

We may recall that when a replacement was sought for Judas Iscariot, Peter stated that the candidates for the position were persons who had accompanied Jesus from the time of his baptism to the day of his ascension. The teaching of the twelve could be completely trusted as the truth since they were Jesus' most intimate companions. Their teaching was considered especially important when erroneous ideas about Jesus began to circulate in the Christian community.

Another foundation of the early church was fellowship. There was a recognition among the early Christians that they could not be Christians in solitude. They needed each other as they dealt with their human frailty and as they shared the spiritual exhilaration of the high moments of their lives. Together they could minister in ways they could never achieve simply as individuals. Throughout Acts it is assumed that Christian faith requires community.

Breaking bread was also an important foundation. In Judaism, breaking bread was associated with some of the most important religious occasions such as the Passover and the Feast of Unleavened Bread (Exodus 12:8, 14–20). Furthermore, every meal for the pious Jew has a certain religious significance and was, therefore, accompanied by a prayer of thanksgiving and a ceremonial breaking of bread. Undoubtedly, Christians continued this custom.

The practice of breaking bread among the early Christians gained added significance in light of the last supper Jesus shared with the twelve and during which he broke bread as a sign of his impending death. It is uncertain whether the breaking of bread mentioned at this point in Acts was actually a celebration of the Lord's Supper or simply a fellowship meal. Whichever it was, it had a profound meaning for the community.

Finally, the early community was devoted to prayer. It followed Jesus' example in recognizing the significance of drawing near to God in this way. We have already seen how important prayer was to the disciples. After Jesus' ascension they all gathered for prayer. They prayed regarding the selection of a new apostle to replace Judas Iscariot. Throughout the rest of Acts there are numerous references to the early Christians engaging in prayer. They offered prayer in their homes, in the temple in Jerusalem, in the synagogue (signs of

27

their continued connection to Judaism), and wherever they were moved to offer praise to God or seek divine guidance. At times they prayed individually. At other times they prayed together. John Wesley, the founder of Methodism, once pointed out that the neglect of prayer was the single most determinative cause of spiritual poverty in the Christian life. The early church found great meaning and energy in the regular practice of prayer.

These were four major features of the life of the early church. But Luke added a few more characteristics to his brief sketch (2:43-47). He said that a sense of awe, of reverence for God, was present in every believer, especially in light of the wonders and signs that God accomplished through the apostles. There was a voluntary sharing of possessions among the members of the community. Since possessions were considered a gift of God, they were to be used when and where there was need. Spirituality and social responsibility were inseparable in the community. When property and personal belongings were sold, there was a common treasury from which funds were distributed to those in need. Later in Acts this common treasury became the focus of additional attention (4:32—5:11; 6:1-6).

Luke closed his description of the principal features of the church's early life in Jerusalem by saying that the disciples found favor with *all* the people, a situation that was to change radically in a very short time as opposition to the Christian movement began to form. In the meantime, however, the community grew as God added to its number.

Acts for Our Time

There are many points at which the events reported by Luke in the first and second chapters of Acts are related to the circumstances of our time. One of the most important is the realization that Jesus' commissioning of the earliest community to be his witnesses is an appointment that we and other apostles share with them. We are witnesses now, not actual eyewitnesses of the resurrection, but witnesses of the power of the Holy Spirit in our lives. Like the earliest disciples, we cannot fulfill the task of Jesus' commission without the divine presence and power of the Holy Spirit among us.

In a book of sermons published several years ago, Halford E. Luccock cited a story about Lorenzo de Medici, the notorious medieval aristocrat and patron of the arts. Lorenzo loved pageants, and the citizens of the Italian city of Florence, his home, enjoyed the realistic spectacles he produced. On one occasion he staged a dramatization of Pentecost in which tongues of actual fire were to descend on the apostles. Unfortunately, the stage and its trimmings were set ablaze by the flames, and to the horror of those present the whole church was soon engulfed in fire and burned to the ground.[3] The power of Pentecost cannot be artificially created by human effort, but its energizing presence, the Holy Spirit, is always a necessity in the Christian community.

We need the Spirit to give us more insight about ourselves. Why are we so satisfied with ourselves and society when we know that God intends us to be different? Why are we content with saying and doing what is safe and popular when the circumstances demand an entirely different and perhaps risky response? While we may not be preoccupied with the date the kingdom will be consummated or fascinated with an event like the ascension, what are the distractions that divert our attention away from the ministry to which all of us are called? The Holy Spirit gives us a better understanding of ourselves.

We need the Spirit to make us one. While we have frequently sung, "We are one in the Spirit; we are one in the Lord," we know how far the Spirit needs to take us before we become the community God intends us to be. We struggle, as did the earliest community, with those forces that inhibit unity and confine our witness, forces such as nationalism, sexism and racism. We need the Spirit to make us one as we serve God and our neighbors.

We need the Spirit to help us to appreciate the gifts we and others possess and to be sensitive to the needs of others in the Christian community and in the larger human family to which we belong. God has given others gifts that enrich our lives and God has blessed us with gifts that can humanize the lives of others. The Spirit can make us more conscious of both the gifts we receive and our opportunities to use our gifts so that the whole human family may be blessed by our mutual sharing.

We need the Spirit to make us bold to speak and to act in love. The Spirit is the "love that will not let [us] go." The Spirit compels us to speak out and to act against that which is contrary to God's will and reminds us that there are resources available to us in the face of evil, fear and despair. The Spirit will give us courage to say and to do that which is right, just and loving.

> O Holy Spirit,
>> Giver of light and life,
> impart to us thoughts higher than our own thoughts,
>> and prayers better than our own prayers,
>> and powers beyond our own powers,
> that we may spend and be spent
> in ways of love and goodness,
>> after the perfect image
>> of our Lord and Savior Jesus Christ. Amen.[4]

Questions and Suggestions

1. The disciples were tempted to become so preoccupied with the question of when the reign of God would come and with the extraordinary religious experience of Jesus' ascension into heaven that they were distracted from the task Jesus had given them. What are the distractions that keep us from fulfilling the work God has for us to do?

2. Was Pentecost a unique event? Are there new Pentecosts in our time?

3. How would you describe the Holy Spirit? What are the evidences of the presence of the Holy Spirit? In what ways is the Holy Spirit at work in your life, in your church, in the world? What is the Spirit leading the church to be and to do?

4. *The Book of Hymns* of The United Methodist Church contains a number of hymns on the Holy Spirit (#131 through #138) and Pentecost (#459 through #467). These and hymns from other collections could be used for study and worship in conjunction with this section of Acts. What do these hymns tell us about the way in which the church has come to understand the Holy Spirit and the Spirit's work among us?

5. Can the early Christian community in Jerusalem with its four foundations (the teaching of the apostles, fellowship, the breaking of bread, and prayer) described in 2:42-47 serve as a valid model for the church today?

6. Baptism is mentioned frequently in Acts beginning with Pentecost. It was not only important in the early church, but it

has remained significant in the church's life to this day. What is the meaning of baptism and how is it connected with who we are and what the church is and does?

7. In many of the speeches delivered by the followers of Jesus in Acts, such as Peter's address on Pentecost, there are quotations from the Old Testament. Why were the Hebrew scriptures (the Old Testament) important to the early Christians? In what ways are they important for the church's witness in our time?

8. In preparation for the next session, read Acts 3:1—5:42.

CHAPTER III

The Community's Ministry and Mounting Opposition
ACTS 3:1—5:42

In the first two chapters of Acts, Luke described the manner in which the disciples of Jesus experienced the presence of the Spirit on Pentecost. He wrote about the immediate results of their receiving the Spirit's power. Under the Spirit's inspiration they spoke in tongues. Peter preached a moving sermon. Many accepted his message and became members of the newly formed community of Jesus' followers. It was a growing community, devoted to learning, worship, fellowship and sharing. Its leaders were the twelve apostles through whom "wonders and signs" were performed. Jesus' followers were viewed favorably by everyone. At this point there was no apparent suspicion of them or opposition to them.

Healing, Arrest and Witness (3:1—4:31)

The story of the early community's ministry and the signs and wonders done through it continued with the narrative of the first healing episode in Acts (3:1–10). As in other places in Acts, Luke did not provide specific information about the time that had elasped between this incident and what immediately preceded it. Given his description of the life of the early community found in 2:42–47, it would appear that he placed this healing story several weeks, if not months, after Pentecost.

Two of the apostles, Peter and John, went to the temple in Jerusalem which was a daily custom of Jesus' followers (2:46).*

---

*Such references remind us that in the beginning, the followers of Jesus considered themselves "the true Judaism."

It was the ninth hour (three o'clock in the afternoon), one of the three times prescribed by the Jewish law for daily prayer. As they entered the temple area by one of its entrances, called the Beautiful Gate, their attention was directed to a crippled beggar who was in his customary place pleading for money. The man was more than forty years of age (4:22) and had been crippled since birth. He asked Peter and John for a gift. Peter's reply was that he had no silver or gold. However, he was willing to give something else. He said to the man, "in the name of Jesus Christ of Nazareth, walk." He reached down and helped the man to his feet. The man's disability vanished. He stood and walked. Accompanied by Peter and John, he entered the temple. His joy was uncontained. He walked and leaped and praised God for being healed. The people who witnessed his ecstatic behavior recognized that he was the crippled beggar who usually sat at the Beautiful Gate. When they realized what had happened to him, they were astounded.

There are several observations to make about this incident. First, it contains four typical elements of a miraculous healing story. (1) It describes a person who needs to be healed. The extent of the person's problem is underscored by a specific description of the condition with which the person is afflicted. In this case, the person cannot walk. Also mentioned is the length of time during which the affliction was present. This man had never walked in his life and he was more than forty years old. (2) The means of healing are stated. In this incident, God's power to heal was mediated through Peter's words, "in the name of Jesus Christ of Nazareth, walk," and his reaching down to touch the crippled man. (3) A confirmation of the healing was made by persons who were witnesses to it. (4) The response to the healing was wonder and amazement.

Second, it is very important to note that for Luke salvation involved the health and well-being of the whole person. Salvation was not confined to the realm of the spiritual alone any more than it was limited to the physical. The spiritual and the physical interact with each other in a way that constitutes the whole person. Therefore, the ministry of Jesus in Luke's Gospel and the ministry of the earliest Christian community in Acts involved both the spiritual and the physical needs of persons (Luke 4:18–19; Luke 5:17–26; Acts 10:36–38).

Third, healings and other types of miracles in Luke's writings were viewed as signs that the kingdom about which Jesus and his followers spoke was actually present in the world. God's reign was becoming a reality in people's lives, even though its completion would take place sometime in the future. The kingdom was not merely something proclaimed in the sermons of the disciples. It was concretely present in the miracles people could see. The combination of word and miraculous deed could evoke faith and result in salvation. Furthermore, the miraculous was evidence of the presence of the Spirit, the energizing power of the kingdom, in the ministry of the apostles and the community in which they were leaders.

The miraculous cure of the lame man was the preparation for another major speech by Peter. According to Luke, a crowd gathered in an area of the temple known as Solomon's Portico. At that spot Peter addressed them. William Neil reminds us of the significance of Peter's words:

> This second speech by Peter is, like his first speech in Chapter 2, of the highest importance for our understanding of how the faith was presented to the Jews in the earliest stage of the Church. In his former address Peter had testified to the power and presence of the Spirit of God at work in a new way in the lives of men [and women] through Jesus. Now he proclaims the power and authority of the name of Jesus by which his disciples are enabled to continue his ministry on earth. In both speeches there is a call for repentance for the crime of crucifying the Messiah, but here Peter stresses the role of Jesus as the Suffering Servant of God and as the new Moses who must be obeyed. The chosen people with whom God has convenanted are challenged to acknowledge Jesus as the fulfillment of ancient prophecy and promises, and are given this chance to return to God before [the] Messiah comes again to bring God's purposes to fruition.[1]

It is worth noting that at the end of his address Peter pointed out that God's servant Jesus had been sent *first* to the descendants of Abraham, Isaac and Jacob to turn them from their wickedness and to bless them. In later speeches in Acts this fact is repeated for the purpose of showing that when Jesus and his message were not widely accepted, the apostles and their companions were directed to go to the Gentiles.

Peter's sermon received a mixed response. Many who heard it "believed," that is, accepted Jesus as the risen Messiah. Others, specifically some of the religious leaders, were annoyed by this unauthorized demonstration in the temple led by Jesus' followers. Priests, the captain of the temple (who was next in rank to the high priest) and Sadducees were especially irritated by the teaching about Jesus and his resurrection from the dead. The Sadducees, whose name meant "righteous ones," were an important group in Judaism for about three hundred years beginning in the second century B.C. They occupied a privileged position with the Romans, were at odds with the Pharisees regarding the interpretation of the Jewish law, and rejected the Pharisees' belief in the resurrection of the dead and the existence of angels. The Sadducees, the priests and the temple captain had Peter and John arrested and imprisoned until the next day when they could be brought before the appropriate authorities.

The next day the two apostles were brought to a hearing, probably a meeting of the Sanhedrin (a council composed of Jewish priests, elders and scribes). Also present were Annas, the former high priest, Caiaphas, the current high priest, and John and Alexander whose identities are difficult to ascertain. The Sanhedrin was a council of seventy leaders who rendered decisions and judgments on various religious and civil issues. Their question to Peter and John was simple: "By what power or by what name did you do this [healing]?"

Peter, prompted and encouraged by the Holy Spirit, replied that what had happened had been done in the name of Jesus Christ of Nazareth. Here, Luke is implying that this response and others like it in Acts fulfilled Jesus' promise that the Holy Spirit would teach his disciples what to say when they were brought before rulers and authorities (Luke 12:11–12). The crucified and risen Jesus was the one responsible for the gift of perfect health to the previously crippled beggar. This Jesus was the cornerstone spoken of in Psalm 118:22 and by Jesus himself in Luke 20:17. Though Jesus had been rejected, he had become the foundation of God's plan of salvation.

Members of the council were impressed by the bold manner of Peter and John as they appeared before them and spoke. After all, these were two common, uneducated men who had stood in the midst of the most powerful religious tribunal in Jerusalem and had claimed that there was salvation in no one other than Jesus. How could the council dispose of the case?

They could not deny that the healing of the crippled beggar had taken place. The whole city knew it. But the preaching about Jesus had to be stopped. The council announced its decision. Peter and John were to be set free, but lest their ideas about Jesus gain wider circulation, they were forbidden to speak or to teach about him. The apostles' reply to the verdict was quick and direct. They could not keep silent about what they had seen and heard. They were compelled to speak out about God's power to heal and to forgive through the risen Christ. The council bristled at this expression of defiance and made additional threats against the two, but was afraid to do harm to them because the people of the city considered the healing of the crippled man a wonderful event and praised God for it. The apostles were released. Their next encounter with the council would be more harsh.

After they had been set free, Peter and John went directly to their friends and reported what had happened to them. They had experienced the first opposition to their ministry, but they had not been harmed. They had dared to defy the authorities and had announced their resolve to speak the truth. They had been sustained by God. It is not surprising, therefore, that the gathered Christian community raised their prayer to God. It was God alone who could endow them with the courage to speak boldly the word of divine judgment and reconciliation. And God alone was the source of power to heal, to perform signs and wonders in the name of Jesus that were the evidences of the divine presence in their work.

As they prayed together, there was something like a second experience of the power of Pentecost. The place where they met began to shake—a typical evidence of God's overwhelming presence (see Exodus 19:18; Isaiah 6:4). Those present experienced a fresh filling of the Holy Spirit, which would inspire them to bear witness to Jesus in their subsequent ministry.

One cannot read this section of Acts without admiring the early Christian community's steadfast loyalty to God. They were just beginning to confront the contempt and threats of those who opposed their work. Their response was neither despair nor fear. They were confident that their words and deeds were in keeping with what God required of them. Furthermore, when they entered into worship together, they were filled with the Spirit and thereby empowered to speak boldly and to perform signs and wonders in the name of Jesus.

The Place of Possessions (4:32—5:11)

At the end of the fourth chapter of Acts there is a brief description of the life of the Christian community, which is similar to the concise account at the conclusion of the second chapter. Luke reemphasized the unity and fellowship that existed in the community. He also reported that the apostles witnessed with great power to God's triumph in the resurrection of Jesus.

In the earlier summary (2:42–47) Luke had mentioned the place of possessions in the life of the community. In section 4:32—5:11, he presented this facet of early Christian life in more detail. Luke reported in both places that Jesus' earliest followers, realizing that their possessions were gifts of God for which they were stewards, voluntarily shared their resources to the extent that no one among them was in need. This sharing was a concrete evidence of the deep sense of harmony and fellowship that existed among them. Theirs was not only a deep spiritual unity, but also a bond that influenced the manner in which they managed and distributed their material resources and cared for those in need.

Sharing one's wealth and caring for the poor was one of the major emphases in Judaism. Writers of the Old Testament had declared that the poor must not be neglected or turned away. Those who gave freely to the needy would be blessed by God (for example, Deuteronomy 15:4–11). Although there were many in need, one of the promises given to the people of Israel was that ultimately there would be no poor among them as God opened their hearts to mutual sharing (Deuteronomy 15:4). Even among the "pagan" philosophers the sharing of possessions was considered an ideal to be pursued. Euripides (fifth century B.C.) had written, "True friends cling not to private property; their wealth is shared in close community." In his *Dialogue on Love* (first century A.D.), Plutarch had said, "Friends possess everything in common."[2] What the Hebrew scriptures and the pagan philosophers held up as the ideal was actually being accomplished in the Christian community.

Even more, the Christians were adhering to Jesus' words and example in their concern for those in need. Jesus had said that it was good to give to the poor (Luke 18:22). Jesus' words, later cited by Paul, proclaimed that "It is more blessed to give than to receive" (Acts 20:35).

According to Luke those who had properties or homes sold them and brought the proceeds to the apostles. The funds were then distributed to persons who needed assistance. The apostles were not merely preachers and teachers; they were also administrators of a common treasury for the welfare of the community.

Luke then offered two illustrations of how members of the community responded to the practice of contributing to the common fund. The first illustration involved Barnabas, one of the most important leaders of the church in the later chapters of Acts. Barnabas was cited as an example of generosity, faithfulness to the standards of the community, and as one led by the Holy Spirit. Barnabas sold a piece of property and brought the proceeds to the apostles as he was expected to do. This was a sign of his self-denial and his concern for others. For Luke, pious persons were also generous persons and their generosity was noteworthy (for example, Tabitha (9:36), Cornelius (10:2) and Paul (24:17).

The second illustration, the story of Ananias and Sapphira, portrayed two members of the community whose apparent greed and attempted deception caused them a tragic end. They had sold some property, but had brought only a part of the proceeds to the apostles. Peter confronted each of them in separate interviews. He accused Ananias of the evil deed. (This Ananias is not to be confused with the Ananias who was involved in Paul's conversion or the Ananias who was the high priest before whom Paul was examined.) Peter charged that like Judas Iscariot (Luke 22:3), Ananias had been filled with Satan rather than the Holy Spirit. Not only had he lied to God, but he had broken faith with the community. Peter asked what had prompted Ananias to such action. There was no recorded reply. Rather, the text reads that Ananias collapsed and died on the spot. Peter's interview with Ananias' wife, Sapphira, followed. After she had admitted her guilt in the incident, she also collapsed at Peter's feet and died. Luke's next line of the story is a classic understatement: "And great fear came upon the whole church and upon all who heard of these things." Is it any wonder!

Ananias and Sapphira had suppressed the leading of the Spirit, and they had betrayed the community to which they belonged. Like Achan in the Old Testament (Joshua 7), they had promised something to God, but were overcome by their own greed. Therefore, according to Luke's account, they reaped the harvest of their hypocrisy.

The ideal of sharing one's resources with those in need continued to be an important practice in the early church. In other places in the New Testament, Christians were exhorted to exhibit their love and care through contributing to the impoverished. One writer stated the case very bluntly: 'If we have the world's goods and see our brothers and sisters in need, yet close our hearts against them, how does God's love abide in us? Let us not love in word or speech but in deed and in truth' (paraphrase of I John 3:17–18). And the ideal of communal sharing, extended beyond the New Testament period into the Christian literature of the second century, seems to imply even more. The writer of the *Letter of Barnabas* wrote, "You shall share everything with your neighbor, and shall not call things your own." In the ethical instructions of the *Didache* (Christian teachings from the second century A.D.), the author advised, "You shall not turn the needy away, but you shall share everything with your brother [and sister], and you shall not say it is your own." Note the concept of common use of all resources.

Luke was persuaded that the way in which the early church dealt with the problem of wealth and poverty among its members was an extremely important facet of the community's life. His interest in this issue is evident not only in this section of Acts, but also in other sections later in the book. Charles H. Talbert has observed that Luke was convinced that

wealth is properly used when it builds relationships and community (Luke 12:33–44; 16:9; Acts 2:44–45; 11:27–30; 24:17). What concerns [Luke] are the social benefits of wealth rightly used. What he wants to avoid is the use of wealth in the service of private indulgence. Moreover, wealth is properly used if the disciples live out of their being filled with the Holy Spirit. Only if they do not follow the Spirit's leading will they use wealth for private indulgence instead of to express and to build community.[3]

For Luke, therefore, wealth was a danger, but it also provided the opportunity for doing good.

The Invincible Work of God (5:12–42)

After his presentation of the place of possessions in the early church, Luke showed how effective the prayers of the community had been. In the section, "Healing, Arrest, and Witness," we noted how the community gathered around Peter and John after they had been released from custody and prayed for boldness to witness and power to heal (4:29–30). Their prayers were answered with a fresh experience of the Holy Spirit. In the present section, the ministry of the apostles continues in the temple area called Solomon's Portico. The first emphasis of the section is on the Spirit's enabling the apostles to perform signs and wonders among the people, especially the healing of the sick.

As word spread about the miraculous deeds accomplished through the apostles' ministry, the astonished populace brought the sick to them for healing. Luke again highlighted the central role of Peter. He claimed that those who required healing were laid on beds and pallets in the streets in order that Peter's shadow would fall on them as he passed by. Furthermore, news about the apostles circulated among the towns near Jerusalem. People from those places brought their sick "and they were all healed" (5:16b).

At the same time the official religious leadership in Jerusalem, which had banned the apostles' witness, also heard about their work. Soon the church's prayers for boldness would be tested in another encounter with the authorities.

Acts states that because of their jealousy, the high priests and the Sadducees* had arrested the apostles and placed them in prison. It is not clear whether the number of those placed in custody included all of the twelve apostles or a smaller group of them. During the night, while they were being held, an angel (messenger) of God appeared, unlocked the doors of the prison, freed them, and instructed them to return to the temple. They were told to resume their witness for "this Life" (5:20). (The term "Life" was probably one of the designations used in the early church to describe the message of salvation and discipleship to which the followers of Jesus were committed.) At daybreak the apostles were teaching in the temple as they had been directed.

*See p. 35 for a description of Sadducees and Pharisees.

Unaware that the apostles had been released from their confinement by divine intervention, the high priest convened the council of the Sanhedrin† to decide what must be done with these prisoners. When officers were sent to bring the apostles to the hearing, it was discovered that they were not in the prison. The prison doors were locked and the sentries were in their places, but the prisoners had vanished.

When the religious leaders were informed about these circumstances, they were surprised and baffled by what had happened. Someone advised them, however, that the prisoners were at that very moment standing in the temple, teaching the people. The apostles were doing exactly what they had been warned not to do. They were sent for and brought to the council without the use of force. A violent arrest might have created a riot since the apostles were apparently popular with the people.

When the apostles arrived for their hearing before the council, they were reminded by the high priest that speaking and teaching about Jesus had been strictly forbidden (4:18). Yet the apostles had defied the prohibition. They had filled the whole city of Jerusalem with their teaching. In a response similar to that offered at the previous hearing before the council (4:19), Peter and his companions stated that they could not abide by the directive of the council because it conflicted with what God had charged them to do.

They were compelled to witness for Jesus who had been unjustly killed, raised from the dead by God, and exalted to God's right hand, the place of highest honor. Jesus had become the leader and savior of Israel. Through him both repentance and the forgiveness of sins were gifts available to God's people. Not only had the apostles been commissioned to proclaim this good news, they had received the Holy Spirit, God's powerful presence, to enable them and all those who obeyed God to testify to the truth.

In this defiant speech by the apostles the church was experiencing the boldness for which it had prayed. There is little doubt that for Luke this divinely inspired and heroic behavior was a sign of God's presence and a model for the whole church to follow when it was threatened by those who were bent on eliminating its life and influence.

---

†A council composed of Jewish priests, elders and scribes.

We can understand why the authorities were enraged by what they considered the apostles' blasphemy. The council was prepared to deal harshly and finally with what to them were the erroneous views of the followers of Jesus. They would kill those who held such views.

One of the members of the council, a rabbi named Gamaliel, highly respected among the Sanhedrin, ordered the apostles removed from the area while he addressed his colleagues. Gamaliel is mentioned only twice in the New Testament. Both references are in Acts. At one place he is pictured as an influential member of the Sanhedrin (5:34). Later in the book he is mentioned as an instructor of Paul (22:3).

According to Luke, Gamaliel was a Pharisee. Like the Sadducees, the Pharisees were one of the most important religious groups in Judaism in Jesus' time. Pharisee, which means "separated one," was an appropriate name for this group since they were very proud of their devotion to the Jewish law and pious practices. Unlike the Sadducees, they did not occupy a privileged position with the Romans. Furthermore, they believed in the resurrection of the dead, a concept not accepted by the Sadducees. There was often vigorous competition between the Pharisees and the Sadducees.

Gamaliel's speech to the council was in the form of a warning. He cautioned them to be very careful about the manner in which they treated the apostles. In fact, he claimed that the best course of action was to keep away from the apostles entirely. History provided two illustrations of trouble-makers whose movements had come and gone without much result. Theudas, a person who made extravagant claims about himself and attracted four hundred followers, was put to death and his disciples were dispersed. His movement was destroyed, Gamaliel observed. Then came Judas the Galilean who had led another uprising. Judas also gathered a following, but his cause was lost when he died and his adherents scattered.

Gamaliel offered advice to the council based on his illustrations. If the movement represented by the apostles was simply a human creation like those of Theudas and Judas, it would fail. Let it alone and it would disappear. On the other hand, if it were a movement with God's blessing and power, nothing could be done to thwart it. Surely, Gamaliel said, his colleagues would not want to be found opposing God's plan.

We have already noted earlier that there is a major problem with Gamaliel's speech. Based on information found in the writings of the reliable Jewish historian Josephus, Judas' uprising occurred about forty years before the movement organized by Theudas. Luke somehow placed them in reverse order. In addition, Josephus placed Theudas' revolt about fifteen years after Gamaliel's address was supposed to have taken place before the council. Luke, therefore, had Gamaliel speaking about an event that had not yet occurred. It is difficult to reconcile the accounts in Josephus with those in Acts. It appears that Luke simply confused the sequence of events. Nevertheless, the logic of the advice he attributed to Gamaliel seemed appropriate, even if the chronology was in error.

According to Luke, Gamaliel was persuasive. The council of the Sanhedrin accepted his counsel. The apostles were summoned. They were ordered again to cease their preaching about Jesus. This time, however, the admonition was accompanied by a beating, probably the forty lashes prescribed for offenses against the law (Deuteronomy 25:3).

The second hearing before the Sanhedrin produced no results different from those of the first. The apostles left the council chamber rejoicing in their suffering. They were following directly in the footsteps of Jesus, the suffering servant, who in the Gospel of Luke proclaims, "Blessed are you when [people] hate you, and when they exclude you and revile you, and cast out your name as evil, on account of the Son of man! Rejoice in that day, and leap for joy, for behold, your reward is great in heaven . . . (Luke 6:22).

Daily in their homes and in the temple the apostles taught and preached Jesus as the Christ, the Messiah, the one through whom sins were forgiven and the gift of the Spirit given. They knew that God's work could not be stopped. The "established order [was] being overwhelmed by the new currents in the unfolding of God's plan."[4]

Acts for Our Time

There are a number of ways in which the chapters of Acts that we have just read and studied speak to the circumstances of our day. We have already mentioned some of them. As we conclude this chapter, it may be helpful to elaborate.

First, we have been reminded that when the early church spoke about salvation it recognized the importance of both the physical and the spiritual life. While the early Christians spoke about the well-being of a person's spirit and the salvation of the soul available through the forgiveness of one's sins, they understood that the state of a person's physical welfare was also critical to salvation. God has constituted each of us as whole persons composed of both body and spirit. The healing of the crippled beggar at the temple gate by Peter and John, and the multiplicity of healings performed by the apostles on other occasions, were not merely signs and wonders to show the power of the Spirit and the presence of the kingdom of God in their midst; those healings also demonstrated divine concern for the physical health of people. During the course of its long history, the Christian church has too frequently yielded to the temptation to minister either to people's spiritual needs or to their physical necessities without realizing that the salvation about which the biblical writers spoke involves both.

Second, questions about the element of the miraculous may be raised by the study of Acts since there are a large number of incidents in the book that might be described as miracles. The healing of the crippled man (3:1–10) and the apostles' release from prison by an angel (5:19) are two examples about which we have read. In the biblical world miracles were widely accepted as unusual interventions by God on behalf of God's people. In more recent times serious questions have been raised about whether it is right to speak about miracles. Some have attempted to give rational explanations to events previously considered miraculous. For example, it might be suggested that the "angel" who was responsible for the apostles' escape from prison in Acts 5:19 was not really a supernatural heavenly being, but merely a human being, a messenger (the Greek word for "angel" means "messenger") who somehow managed to assist the apostles in their flight from confinement.

How are we to regard the various divine judgments and miracles in Acts? Obviously, this is a question about which more could be said than space allows in this book. While some of the events described by Luke as miracles or divine judgments may have for us a more reasonable explanation, we do the author of Acts a grave disservice if we dismiss them as expressions of a primitive mentality. One of his reasons for including the miracle and judgment stories was to show that God can and does intervene in human affairs in extraordinary ways. Reason has an appropriate role in analyzing what takes place around us and in seeking to understand the ways of God. Luke would add, so does mystery!

Third, it is humbling to note that in Acts the opposition to the ministry of the early church principally came from the established religious leadership. It began with those who were considered by others and who considered themselves to be the more theologically informed and devout persons of their day. Yet this group had become so locked into certain theological views and religious practices that they were unable to grasp the new directions in which God was moving to enrich their lives.

It is frightening to contemplate the idea that we might be tempted to dismiss or deal harshly with persons who might be witnesses to God's new directions in our time. We need to consider with great care, sound theological judgment, and much prayer the new options God may be setting before us through the witness of others, for the sake of a more abundant life for us and for all of our neighbors. Gamaliel's words are a warning to us. We must be careful lest we be found opposing God.

Fourth, the members of the early Christian community were undaunted by opposition to their witness. They were neither discouraged nor fearful in the face of extremely hazardous situations. Convinced that they were doing God's will, they lived out of resources beyond themselves. They discovered strength in the presence of God and in the mutual encouragement of their sisters and brothers. The love and prayers of the community were their constant support during periods of severe testing. They were not intimidated by any civil or religious authority they identified as being contrary to God's reign in the world.

In their first encounters with the opposition, the followers of Jesus suffered verbal and physical abuse. In later meetings with their antagonists, some of them, like Stephen and the apostle James, would become martyrs. The Greek term *martus* from which the English word "martyr" is derived, means "faithful witness." Some would be faithful to death. But even the prospect of execution was not sufficient to keep them from naming the evils around them, calling for repentance, and offering new life through Christ. They set a worthy example for their successors, including us.

Questions and Suggestions

1. Luke made it clear that the early church was not only concerned about the salvation of people's souls, but also about their health and physical well-being. In what ways does the church express its continuing concern for health and health care? What is the role of the church as a healing community? In what ways may we be the bearers of Jesus' healing presence?

2. According to Luke, miracles, signs and wonders occurred in the early church. How would you define "miracle"? Is it reasonable to believe that miracles still happen?

3. One of the ways the early Christians demonstrated that an intimate bond of fellowship and love existed among them was through the mutual sharing of their possessions. They had everything in common and there was not a needy person among them. Why? How can we use our possessions to build up the Christian community? How well are we providing for the needs of our sisters and brothers in the church and beyond the church? What do you think Luke intended to teach with the story of Ananias and Sapphira?

4. Christians in the early church were called to be witnesses to the resurrection of Jesus. Why is the resurrection important?

5. What do you think about Gamaliel's counsel to the Sanhedrin that they should not interfere with the new religious and social movement represented by Peter and the apostles? While his advice worked to the benefit of those on trial, is there any danger in our adopting Gamaliel's philosophy in the decisions we face?

6. What risks confront Christians today in various parts of the world as they seek to be faithful to their commission to be witnesses for the love, power and justice of God?

7. In preparation for the next session, read Acts 6:1—9:31.

CHAPTER IV

The Gospel vs.
Traditional Ideas and Barriers
ACTS 6:1—9:31

The leaders of the early Christian community, the apostles, had taken their message about God's acts in Jesus to the temple, the most important religious place in Judaism, and to the Sanhedrin, the most influential religious assembly among the Jews. They had proclaimed Jesus as the Holy and Righteous One of God, the Author of life, Leader and Savior, God's servant, the Christ (Messiah). The apostles called on all those who heard their preaching to turn away from their sins and evil deeds and promised God's forgiveness to those who sought it. As a sign of the salvation and wholeness available through Jesus they also performed healings in his name. The results of this ministry were evident. A growing number of people were being attracted to the Christian fellowship.

Furthermore, the apostles were the leading personalities in a community of Jesus' followers organized for nurture and committed to generous mutual sharing. The community lived daily in the power of the Spirit, seeking to please God and to extend the community's witness. Despite the opposition that formed against it, the church, as presented to us in Acts, was determined that by the grace of God it would not merely survive, but would fulfill the commission to be Jesus' witnesses in Jerusalem, throughout Judea and Samaria, and to the end of the earth. It was confident that with the leading of the Spirit it could confront tensions and problems within its fellowship and

47

withstand the pressures and difficulties brought to bear on it from its opponents. With God's help it might even witness the conversion of some of its most feared antagonists.

Neglect and Remedy (6:1–7)

In this section Luke described a problem that emerged in the Christian community at Jerusalem. As the church was growing, some of its widows were not receiving what they needed to exist on a daily basis. They were being neglected. This situation was very serious because a widow's status in the ancient world was usually quite precarious. Very often, when their husbands died, widows were left without property or income. They had no other option than to rely on the charity of others. In Old Testament times the plight of the widow was considered of special concern to God. Therefore, the law provided for the care of widows (Deuteronomy 14:28–29). The prophets exhorted the people of Israel to furnish the needs of widows and warned of God's displeasure when they were neglected or mistreated (for example, Isaiah 1:16–17, 21–25). Widows were to receive the compassionate attention of God's people. This same concern for the widow was continued in the early church. It was part of the sharing described in Acts 2:44–45 and 4:32–34. But it wasn't working. Some of the widows in the church were being overlooked in the daily distribution from the treasury administered by the apostles.

The problem was aggravated by the fact that it was only the Hellenists' widows who were being ignored. The Hellenists, Greek-speaking Jewish Christians, complained that the Hebrews, who were Aramaic-speaking Jewish Christians, were responsible for this situation. Although the negligence appeared to be unintentional, it involved a discriminatory practice within the church that could destroy the common fellowship and ministry characteristic of the presence of the Holy Spirit in their midst. Furthermore, how could the community witness effectively in Jerusalem, not to mention to the end of the earth, if it was insensitive to the needs of its own members!

The leaders of the church knew that this problem had to be solved as quickly as possible. They assembled the community and proposed a remedy for the situation. Since the twelve felt that they were unable to fulfill their preaching and teaching responsibilities while properly managing the church's relief funds, they suggested that the community select seven persons to administer its charitable resources. These persons should have good reputations, possess wisdom, and be filled with the presence and power of God. Following their selection by the community, the apostles would appoint them to their special task. This would permit the twelve to continue to devote themselves to prayer and preaching.

The community concurred with the apostles' proposal and chose seven persons: Stephen, Philip, Prochorus, Nicanor, Timon, Parmenas, and Nicolaus. Since these seven persons had Greek names, they probably belonged to the group of Hellenists in the church who felt that their widows had been the objects of the church's discrimination. These seven Greek-speaking Jewish Christians represented the interests of those who were oppressed.

They were brought to the apostles who prayed for them and laid their hands on their heads. The laying on of hands was a ritual that invested the seven men with special authority and power to perform the task for which they had been selected. One commentator has said about this incident, "The problem of unintentional structural injustice [in the church was] remedied by the recognition of a diversity of gifts and functions within the church's leadership and by the recognition that every segment of the community's membership needs to be represented in that leadership."[1]

Luke concluded his description of the neglect of the widows and the church's solution to that problem with a statement implying that the church's action in the matter was correct. In settling the dispute between the Hellenists and the Hebrews and redesigning the structure and composition of its ministry, the church's witness was made more effective and it continued to grow rapidly in Jerusalem. An ever larger group of people was drawn into its life, including some priests from the temple.

Stephen—the First Martyr (6:8—8:1a)

Luke devoted a very large section of Acts to the witness and martyrdom of Stephen. Stephen had been previously mentioned as one of the seven chosen to insure the proper care of the widows of the Hellenists. He was the only person in that list of seven whose credentials were cited by Luke. He was called "a man full of faith and of the Holy Spirit" (Acts 6:5). Stephen was also the first significant member of the early Christian community to occupy a prominent place in Acts who was not one of the twelve.

Stephen's story can be divided into three main parts. In the first part (6:8—7:1) Luke told his readers that Stephen spoke with wisdom and the Spirit and that he performed signs and wonders (like the apostles and other disciples). He was a person filled with the grace and power of God. His witness, however, moved some to argue with him about his testimony. Those who disputed with Stephen were members of one of the synagogues in Jerusalem, the synagogue to which belonged former Jewish prisoners or descendants of those prisoners from Cyrene, Alexandria, Cilicia and Asia who had been freed by their Roman captors.

Stephen's adversaries were no match for him. They could not compete with his wisdom because he was led by the Spirit. Since his opponents were unable to gain any advantage over him in regular debate, they decided to employ devious means to bring him to the attention of the authorities.

A plot was devised to have Stephen punished for his words and deeds. The schemers engaged a group of men who accused Stephen of showing contempt and lack of reverence for God and Moses. They stirred up so much trouble among the people and religious leaders that Stephen was seized and brought before the Sanhedrin for a hearing. Furthermore, witnesses were brought to the hearing who would testify that Stephen spoke against the temple and the law God had given to the people of Israel. According to Luke similar charges were later lodged against Paul (Acts 21:28; 25:8).

As the council looked at Stephen, they saw that his face was like that of one of God's messengers (angels). Like the face of Moses at Mount Sinai (Exodus 34:29–35), Stephen's countenance indicated that he was one uniquely near to God.

The scene had been set. Stephen had been charged in the presence of the Sanhedrin. He had been accused of antagonism to both the temple and the law. The high priest, who presided over the council, asked Stephen whether the charges against him were true. We have been prepared to hear Stephen's defense.

50

The second part of the story (7:2–53) consists of Stephen's speech to the Sanhedrin. It is the longest speech in Acts, and contains Stephen's answer to the accusations of his adversaries. It is basically a summarization of some of the most important phases of Old Testament history. The names and deeds of the ancient leaders of God's people are recorded—Abraham, Isaac, Jacob, Joseph, Moses, Aaron, Joshua, David, Solomon, and the prophets.

The purpose in reviewing history in this way was to make clear at least two facts. First, although God had repeatedly provided outstanding leaders for the people of Israel throughout their history, the people had consistently refused to acknowledge those who conveyed God's word to them. They had even willfully disobeyed the law God had given. Second, although they had constructed a tabernacle, the tent of witness, in the wilderness and had later built the temple in Jerusalem, both of which were to enable the people to worship more faithfully, the people had become idolaters and erroneously believed that God's presence was somehow limited to the structures they had erected.

So, Stephen alleged, he was not acting against the law and the temple. Rather, it was the people of Israel who had a long history of breaking the law, persecuting its defenders, and misunderstanding the purpose of the structures built to worship God. In the final sentences of his address Stephen was sharply critical of those who had attacked him. Like their ancestors, they resisted the inspiration and guidance of the Spirit of God. They had even betrayed and murdered Jesus, the Righteous One of God. Stephen had turned the tables on his foes. The accusers stood accused.

The third part of the story about Stephen (7:54—8:1a) describes the results of Stephen's speech. The reaction of the council to Stephen was predictable and similar to its response to the speech of Peter and the apostles (5:33). The Sanhedrin was furious and desired to see Stephen appropriately punished for his offensive words. Luke reported that at that very moment Stephen had a vision of heaven in which he saw Jesus standing at God's right hand, the place of exalted authority. As the council continued to express its rage against Stephen, he told them about his vision of the exalted Christ who now occupied the place of greatest favor with God. Stephen's claim of Jesus' exaltation simply intensified the anger of the council. They refused to hear any more of his blasphemous words. He was seized and dragged out of the city to be executed for blasphemy according to the provisions of the law (Deuteronomy 13:6–11; Leviticus 24:10–16).

The law prescribed that the guilty party should be stoned to death not only as punishment for alleged offenses against God, but to show others that they, too, would come to such an end if they taught contemptible and erroneous ideas. Acts makes no mention of the assent of the Roman authorities to Stephen's execution, though their approval was usually required for such action.

Stonings usually occurred outside of a city. The accused was stripped of clothing and usually thrown from a height or dropped into a pit. The witnesses who had testified were the first to roll or throw large rocks at the accused. Then the rest of those present were encouraged to join the ceremony. Cumbersome clothing was removed by those hurling the stones so that they could increase the velocity and accuracy of their throws. The stoning did not cease until the offender had been killed.

This was the fate of Stephen, one of the seven, a person filled with the Holy Spirit. The words attributed to Jesus in Luke 21:16 had been fulfilled: ". . . some of you they will put to death." Stephen's last acts are certainly reminiscent of Jesus' deeds as he was being crucified. Luke portrays Stephen's death as parallel in many ways to that of Jesus. He prayed for his executioners (compare Luke 23:34 with Acts 7:60), and he committed his spirit into the hands of the heavenly powers (compare Luke 23:46 with Acts 7:59). Luke reported that Stephen "fell asleep," a characteristic way of describing one's death in the New Testament.

At the scene of Stephen's execution we are introduced to a new character in Acts. His name was Saul. Luke said that he was the guardian of the clothing removed by those who stoned Stephen. Furthermore, Saul approved of Stephen's execution. There is not a hint here that this accomplice to Stephen's murder would soon experience a profound tranformation and become the most illustrious missionary in the early church, if not in the whole history of Christianity.

Persecution and Opportunity (8:1b–40)

Luke reported that on the very day of Stephen's death a widespread and intense persecution of the church in Jerusalem was initiated. Although he did not describe the details of the persecution, it must have been severe because the members of the community began to flee the city. Only the apostles remained. It is not clear why they chose to stay. It has been suggested that the apostles may have been considered less radical than other elements in the church and, therefore, not a great threat to the established religious order. Or, perhaps they remained as a sign of their resolve that in spite of persecution they would not be driven away from the work God had given them to do in Jerusalem.

Among those who attempted to destroy the church by intimidating and brutalizing its members was Saul who took a leading role in the persecution. He went through the streets of the city dragging Christians from their homes and taking them to prison.

According to Luke, the persecution of the church in Jerusalem was the first systematic attempt to eliminate the life and witness of the earliest Christian community. As we shall see, however, it had the opposite effect. As the followers of Jesus scattered into Judea and Samaria, they carried with them their testimony to God's judgment and grace in the life, death, resurrection and exaltation of their Leader and Savior. As Talbert observes, "In trying to beat out the flames of Christianity, its opponents had scattered sparks far and wide and only increased the scope of the fire."[2] Throughout Acts persecution offered opportunity for the faithful to bear witness to God's love and power in their words and deeds.

Luke provided three illustrations of the way in which the scattering of the church aided the extension of its ministry.

In the first illustration (8:4–8) Philip, who was one of the seven appointed to supervise the contributions to the widows (6:5), went into Samaria to proclaim the message about Jesus and to engage in healing the sick. In one of the towns of Samaria, Philip was especially successful in his work. Many welcomed his preaching and were impressed by the mysterious deeds he performed. They were joyous because of what they heard and saw.

What makes this incident about Philip unusually important is where it took place—in Samaria. This is the first recorded instance of the Christian message being taken to, and received by, Samaritans. Samaria was the central hill country lying between Judea and Galilee. Its inhabitants were regarded by the Jews as despicable and unbelieving. The Jews were critical of the mixed ancestry of the Samaritans and their claim that Mount Gerizim in Samaria, and not Jerusalem, was the most sacred place to worship God.

Hostility between Jews and Samaritans was intense in Jesus' time. Dealings between the two were discouraged. It was scandalous to his Jewish listeners when Jesus made a Samaritan the hero of one of his parables (Luke 10:29–37). Despite the antagonism that existed between the Jews and the people of Samaria, Philip, a Jewish Christian, had set out on a mission to the Samaritans. And he had been successful. Philip stated that God's salvation embraced even the Samaritans and they were invited to participate fully in the community of Christ.

Adhering to Jesus' instructions (1:8), the testimony of his followers, begun in Jerusalem, had now been extended to Judea and to Samaria. The gospel was breaking down traditional ideas and barriers that had existed for centuries. It was replacing them with the good news that God's love and power were available to everyone, especially through a community whose membership was open to all.

Luke's second illustration (8:9–25) also occurred in the territory of Samaria. It involved a man named Simon who had practiced magic and had claimed that he possessed great power. Simon amazed people with his mystifying deeds. This is the first of three places in Acts in which the practice of magic is mentioned. The others are 13:6–8 and 19:19. In the ancient world magic included the methods by which the magician attempted to manipulate and control divine forces to do what the magician wanted them to do. Magic was strongly criticized in the Old Testament (Deuteronomy 18:10–12; Isaiah 47:12–15) and Acts reflects a similar position. God's power cannot be controlled to entertain others, to glorify oneself, or to attain one's selfish desires.

When the people who had previously been impressed with Simon's magic heard Philip's message about the kingdom of God and God's powerful witness in Jesus, they believed and were baptized, both men and women. By Luke's account, even Simon believed, was baptized, and accompanied Philip in his work. But, as we shall see later (8:18–24), the story of Simon's conversion is not an altogether satisfactory one. Luke does not make it clear whether his conversion, in the end, was a true one, or whether he was simply trying to acquire for his own money-making use powers that he saw at work through Philip. Luke's final word about Simon in 8:24 is that he asked Peter to pray for him.

The news about Philip's success in Samaria was carried back to the apostles in Jerusalem. They decided that they should send a delegation to confirm the reports they had received and to pray for the new disciples in order that they might receive the Holy Spirit. Although the new converts had been baptized with water, they had not yet received the special filling of God's presence and power that had been conferred on the church at Pentecost. Peter and John were dispatched to the Samaritan Christians. When they arrived in Samaria, they laid their hands on the new members of the community and they were filled with the Spirit. When Simon, the magician, saw the results of the laying on of hands by the apostles, he offered them money so that he might acquire the ability to convey the Spirit in the same fashion. Peter scolded Simon for thinking that a gift of God could be bought with money. He asked whether Simon had lapsed into his old way of acting as a magician. Did he believe that God's power could be purchased and controlled for his own benefit? Peter demanded that Simon turn from this wicked intent. His desire to acquire spiritual authority was a sign that he was not yet completely free from his fascination with magic. Simon acknowledged his wrong and requested prayer on his behalf. For many centuries the practice of buying and selling positions in the church has been called "simony," a reminder of this episode in Acts.

Peter and John concluded their visit with the new members of the church in the Samaritan community in which Philip worked. On their way back to Jerusalem they proclaimed the Christian message in several villages of Samaria. Work among the Samaritans had now received the apostolic seal of approval.

The third and final illustration of the extension of the church's ministry resulting from the scattering caused by persecution is the story of Philip and the Ethiopian eunuch

(8:26–40). According to Luke, Philip was divinely led to travel to a desert road running south from Jerusalem to Gaza, a town near the Mediterranean coast. On that road he met an Ethiopian eunuch who had visited and worshipped in Jerusalem. The eunuch was returning to his own land south of Egypt. He was the treasurer for the Ethiopian ruler Candace whose hereditary title meant "queen-mother."

Eunuchs were men who had been castrated. Their testicles had either been removed or crushed, usually in order to guarantee that they could be trusted as the guards of the royal harems. The Jewish law excluded a eunuch from entering the temple, the sacred assembly of God (Deuteronomy 23:1). Thus, by virtue of a physical deformity, the eunuch, though he was probably a Jew, was not entitled to full rights in the Jewish religious community. Nevertheless, Luke portrayed him as a prayerful person who was interested in the scriptures. He had worshipped in Jerusalem and as he rode in his chariot he was reading aloud the Hebrew scriptures.

The Spirit prompted Philip to approach the eunuch's chariot and to join him as he traveled. The eunuch invited Philip to help him understand a section of Isaiah that he had been reading. It was a section of the Old Testament frequently cited by the writers of the New Testament, Isaiah 53, one of the Servant Songs. The eunuch asked Philip whether the "servant" described in Isaiah 53 was Isaiah himself or someone else. Philip "told him the good news of Jesus." The eunuch was so moved by Philip's testimony that he had his chariot stopped and requested that Philip baptize him. As they came up out of the water, Luke tells us, "the Spirit of the Lord caught up Philip, and the eunuch saw him no more." The eunuch continued on his journey with great joy, and Philip appeared next at Azotus, a town west of Jerusalem near the Mediterranean coast. From Azotus he traveled north to Caesarea preaching in the towns along the way.

The point of the story of Philip and the Ethiopian is clear. While the eunuch could never enjoy full privileges and rights under the old covenant of Israel because he was a eunuch, he was free to possess the complete benefits of the new covenant instituted by Christ including membership in the church. Another traditional idea and barrier had been broken by the gospel.

Talbert has correctly observed that the thrust of this chapter in Acts, "is that all sorts of people are included in God's people: Samaritans, eunuchs, women as well as men, magicians as well as those impressed by magic. All can believe in Jesus, all can be baptized, all can receive the gift of the Holy Spirit, all can be fully included in the church."[3]

A Dramatic and Incredible Change (9:1–31)

According to the narrative in Acts, no opponent of the early church was more determined to suppress it than Saul. He was introduced to the readers of the book as the person who not only desired Stephen's death, but also guarded the clothing of those who stoned him (7:58; 8:1). Furthermore, Saul was at the center of the campaign to persecute the Christians in Jerusalem. He ravaged the church, dragging men and women from their homes and having them consigned to prison (8:1–3). Saul's villainous crusade continued as Luke pictured him at the beginning of the eighth chapter threatening to kill the followers of Jesus not only in Jerusalem, but as far away as Damascus. Luke reported that Saul attempted to secure letters from the high priest in Jerusalem introducing him to the synagogues of Damascus and authorizing him to seize any followers of Jesus who might have fled to that city.

It is important to note that Christianity is described in this section as "the Way" (9:2). There are five other places in Acts where Luke used this designation for the early Christian community (19:9, 23; 22:4; 24:14; 24:22). Note Jesus' reference to himself as "the way" to a new relationship with God (John 14:4–6) and, consequently, to a new way of life.

Apparently, Saul secured the letters which he had sought from the high priest. He set off for Damascus intent on inflicting as much damage as possible on the Christians who resided there. But in one of the most dramatic and incredible episodes in Acts, Saul was stopped from carrying out his purpose.

Luke described the circumstances of Saul's experience on his way to Damascus in this way: As he approached Damascus, "a light flashed about him." Saul suddenly fell to the ground, and he heard a voice inquiring of him, "Why do you persecute me?" In verse 6, the voice is identified as that of Jesus who then instructs Paul to continue his journey into Damascus where he will receive further directions concerning what he is to do. Since he had been blinded, Saul was led into the city by those who were traveling with him. For the next three days he neither ate nor drank. Perhaps the overpowering nature of his experience with the risen Christ had left him so shaken that he had no appetite. As a devout Jew, he also might quite naturally have chosen to fast.

One of the Christians living in Damascus was a devout man named Ananias. He is not to be confused with the Ananias who died after his confrontation with Peter (5:1–6) or Ananias the high priest who appeared later in Acts (23:2, 24:1). In a vision, this Ananias was instructed by the Lord to find Saul. Saul had already been shown that Ananias would search for him. When Ananias found Saul, he was told that he should lay hands on him and that Saul would regain his sight.

We can imagine Ananias' shock when he was given these instructions. By that time Saul was notorious. News about his violent treatment of Jesus' followers in Jerusalem and his intention to harm the Christians in Damascus had circulated widely. Seeking out the wicked Saul and serving as a means by which his blindness would be cured was the most unpleasant task Ananias could have been asked to perform. Like Jonah of centuries before, Ananias was being asked to go into the camp of the enemy. It is not surprising that he was both stunned and reluctant to undertake the task. The instructions, however, came a second time. Ananias must go because Saul, the most vigorous foe of the church, had been chosen to become the witness of God's salvation in Christ to the Gentiles, to royalty, and to the people of Israel (9:15). Ironically, the very person who was the leader of the crusade to abolish the Christian community had been elected to be a missionary who would suffer for the cause he had tried so diligently to eliminate.

Ananias did as he was told. He found Saul and with grace that is breathtaking under the circumstances, Ananias did two things. First, he laid his hands on Saul, thereby conferring God's blessing and the promise of the Holy Spirit on the archenemy of the church. Second, he addressed him as "Brother Saul," a greeting that indicated a new relationship, instituted by God, not only between Saul and Ananias, but also between Saul and the whole church. Saul's sight was restored. He was baptized, and regained his strength for the work ahead.

Luke did not describe any of the details or problems surrounding Saul's acceptance by the followers of Jesus in Damascus. Perhaps many of them wondered whether his conversion was authentic. Any doubts probably began to vanish as Saul entered the synagogues in Damascus and proclaimed Jesus as the Son of God. The change that had taken place in him also mystified those outside the Christian community. They found it difficult to believe that the most notorious persecutor of the church had become a disciple of Jesus. Luke underscored the effectiveness of Saul's testimony by remarking that he argued persuasively that Jesus was the Christ (Messiah), and that he was so convincing that the "Jews of Damascus plotted to kill him." Note that in II Corinthians 11:32–33, it was the governor (civil authority) who "guarded the city in order to sieze him." In both references, those who opposed his teachings were at the gates of the city to attack him when he left. However, when Saul learned of their intention, he escaped from Damascus with the help of his disciples who lowered him from the city wall in a basket during the night.

Luke made no reference to Saul's (Paul's) own claim that following his conversion he spent three years in Arabia before going to Damascus and then to Jerusalem (Galatians 1:17–18). According to Luke, Saul traveled from Damascus to Jerusalem where he desired to meet with other disciples. The Christians in Jerusalem, however, were skeptical about his recent embracing of their faith. They were afraid of Saul and may have thought that he was pretending to be a disciple in order to create even more trouble for the church.

Barnabas, one of the members of the church in Jerusalem, spoke to the apostles on behalf of Saul. He described Saul's experience on the road to Damascus and told about his bold and effective preaching in the city. Barnabas was prepared to welcome and defend someone whom the rest of the church still regarded with fear and uncertainty. His endorsement of Saul persuaded the apostles that Saul was a genuine disciple. Thereafter, Saul began to preach the Christian message in Jerusalem.

When certain Greek-speaking Jews threatened to kill Saul because of his preaching, other disciples took him to the port of Caesarea and sent him off to Tarsus, his home town in Asia Minor. This was the last mention of Saul until Barnabas went to find him in order to enlist his services for missionary work in Antioch (11:25). In the meantime, it may be presumed that Saul was engaged in preaching the Christian message in his home territory.

This section of Acts in which Luke told the story of Saul's dramatic and incredible change is one of the most important parts of the book. It explains how an avowed enemy of the followers of Jesus was transformed into an enthusiastic advocate of the Way. Saul, later in Acts called Paul, became a key personality in the second half of Acts and the outstanding leader of the church's work among the Gentiles. Luke emphasized the amazing change that took place in Saul's life not only by telling the story of his conversion in this section of the book, but also by retelling it twice in later places (22:3–16; 26:9–18). Paul also recounted the incident in one of his letters (Galatians 1:11–24). There are differences between Paul's account in Galatians and the accounts in Acts, even as there are differences in the three versions in Acts, but the significance of the story is in the change that took place in Paul.

Luke closed this part of the book with another of his characteristic summary statements in which he described the faithfulness, welfare, and growth of the church (9:31; compare with 2:43–47; 4:32–33; 5:12–16). He had shown some of the ways in which the Christian message had broken down traditional ideas and barriers of race, culture, sex, physical condition, and theology for the sake of a community devoted to God's love, power and justice. He was convinced that when the church did as God intended, its life was strengthened and its ministry was made more effective.

Acts for Our Time

These chapters in Acts contain a number of themes pertinent to the Christian community in our time.

One of them is the issue of martyrdom. Unfortunately, though Stephen's death was the first martyrdom in the history of Christianity, it was not the last. He was merely one of a long succession of men and women who were to be martyred for the sake of their faithfulness to Christ and the Way. From the first to the twentieth century A.D., there have been countless Christians who have lost their lives at the hands of others because they were unwilling to surrender to forces they considered contrary to the purpose of God. Some of them have been our contemporaries. We are familiar with the stories of Dietrich Bonhoeffer, Martin Luther King, Jr., and Archbishop Oscar Romero.

The names and stories of other Christian martyrs are not as well known or well remembered. In December of 1980, four American Roman Catholic women, three nuns and one lay volunteer, disappeared while driving from San Salvador's airport to a mission in La Libertad, El Salvador. Their burned-out van was found, and their missing bodies were discovered in a crude grave twenty-five miles southeast of San Salvador. Sister Dorothy Kazel of the Ursuline Order and Jean Donovan, a lay volunteer, both from Cleveland, along with two Maryknoll sisters, Ita Ford and Maura Clarke, were victims of those who opposed their solidarity with Salvadoran people seeking basic human rights. They are twentieth century martyrs to the cause of justice and peace. See also the story of Fannie Lou Hammer in the 1986 spiritual growth study book, *Hallelujah Anyhow!* by Diedra Kriewald, p. 53 ff. (listed in "Resources," p. 126.)

Herman Stohr was a teacher in Germany during the most powerful years of the Hitler regime. His Christian commitment inspired him to oppose Naziism and to write, organize, and teach about the welfare and peace of the whole human race. On June 21, 1940 Stohr was martyred by the Nazis for the ideals he had stated early in his life and by which he had lived all his life:

Love, as it is made manifest in the life and death of Christ, is the only power that can conquer evil and the only enduring foundation for human society. In order to establish a world order based on love, those who believe in this fundamental principle must themselves completely accept it. They must assume the consequences that arise in a world that does not yet recognize this order.[4]

The stories of the martyrs—of Stephen, of Hermann Stohr, of other Christians imprisoned, tortured and perhaps dying for their faith today—raise most important questions for us. What is worth risking our lives to see accomplished for the sake of God's reign and the welfare of the human race? When we answer the question about what we are willing to die for, perhaps we can determine what we are willing to live for.

A second issue concerns the inclusive nature of the membership of the early church. One of the major questions the church faced in its earliest years had to do with who was invited to belong to it and who could participate fully in its life. Jesus, of course, had already set the example in his servant ministry to all types of people including those who were generally neglected by the official religious establishment of his time.

The early Christian community embraced all sorts of people. Race, sex, ethnicity, physical condition and economic status, which were barriers preventing certain persons from full participation in some quarters of the religious and social community of the ancient world, were broken by repentance and faith in Christ. The Way was open to everyone.

In the Constitution of The United Methodist Church (Division One, Article 4) the denomination recognizes that as "a part of the Church Universal, which is one Body in Christ, . . . "all persons, without regard to race, color, national origin, or economic condition, shall be eligible to attend its worship services, to participate in its programs, and, when they take the appropriate vows, to be admitted into its membership in any local church in the connection." At every place in its life and leadership the church is required by the Spirit to include all who confess Jesus Christ as Lord and who are the recipients of the gifts of the Spirit. Anything less is heresy of the heart.

A third issue is raised by the complete change that God worked in the life of Saul of Tarsus. Of all the men and women who were prospects for membership in the earliest Christian community, Saul was the least likely. He passionately hated the followers of Jesus and everything they represented. He actively worked for their destruction. Yet, God's love pursued him. God would not let him go. The most improbable candidate for Christian discipleship was so thoroughly changed by God that he became the foremost missionary for Christ in the early church.

We dare not limit the potential of the gospel and the power of the Spirit to change people. Those whose deeds seem to us to be totally contrary to God's will and the welfare of the whole human community may be completely transformed by God's grace. The least likely should be included in our prayers. The caring ministry of the church should reach out to them. There is always new life with fresh possibilities where Jesus Christ is Lord.

Questions and Suggestions

1. The widows of the Hellenists (the Greeks) were among the most helpless members of the early Christian community. Why? How do you feel about the manner in which the church corrected the problem of their being neglected? Who are those most likely to be neglected or ignored in the church? What can be done to insure that they are treated justly?

2. Why does persecution seem to strengthen the church? Where is the persecution of Christians occurring in the world at present? When faced with opposition, trouble and danger, should the Christian resist or "bend with the wind?" What are some of the key issues for which Christians are being persecuted?

3. Can Stephen serve as an example for today's Christian? Have one or more persons in the group briefly tell the group about two or three recent Christian martyrs. (See p. 61. Also check issues of *Response* and *New World Outlook*.) Compare the stories of the modern martyrs with Stephen. What lessons do the martyrs have to teach us?

4. In Luke's time, magic, practiced by people like Simon, represented an attempt to control divine forces for the benefit and power of a relatively small group of people. In what ways are individuals, nations, and social and religious groups tempted to claim control of God's presence and power for their own purposes?

5. In the episode regarding the conversion of the Ethiopian eunuch what roles did the following have: Philip, the Holy Spirit, the scriptures?

6. One of the major emphases in this section of Acts and in the next is that those considered the least likely prospects to receive God's grace and become members of the Christian community (Samaritans, magicians, eunuchs, persecutors, Gentiles) became Christian disciples and full participants in the life of the church. Depending on our race, color, nationality, economic class and other factors, we are tempted to identify the

people most unlike us as the least likely to be our sisters and brothers in Christ. Who are they? Is it difficult to think of Christians in the Soviet Union as our sisters and brothers in Christ? Does common faith in Christ transcend the traditional ideas and barriers that keep us apart?

7. Ask someone to read the story of Heliodorus in II Maccabees 3 (in the Apocrypha) and compare it for the group with the account of Paul's conversion in Acts. Are there similarities between the two stories? What do you think about sudden and incredible conversions like Paul's? Why are we tempted to limit the potential of the gospel to change people?

8. Compare the three accounts of Paul's conversion in Acts (9:1–22; 22:3–16; 26:9–18) with each other and with Paul's own account in Galatians 1:11–17. What are the similarities and differences among them? Can you suggest reasons for the differences?

9. In preparation for the next session of the group, ask participants to read Acts 9:32—21:16.

CHAPTER V

The Advance of the Gospel
ACTS 9:32—21:16

The early Christians received divine power and they were Jesus' witnesses in Jerusalem, Judea and Samaria. Jesus' promise to his followers was being fulfilled as they surrendered themselves to the course the Spirit was setting for them. The church seemed ready to complete the mission Jesus had outlined before his ascension and exaltation. Having born testimony in Jerusalem, Judea and Samaria, the church was now prepared to take the gosepl "to the end of the earth" (1:8). To do that it had to cross the most significant obstacle it had thus far encountered. It had to convey the good news about Jesus and introduce the Way to the Gentiles.

The term "Gentile" comes from the Latin word *gens*, which means "nation." In the Bible, "Gentile" simply refers to someone who is not Jewish.

The attitudes and relationships between Jews and Gentiles in the centuries before Christ were mixed. One Old Testament prophet believed that God had chosen Israel to be "a light to the nations" (Isaiah 42:6 and 60:3). Through the witness of Israel, Gentiles would be invited to participate with Jews in the blessings of God's reign. Other Old Testament authors, such as Ezra and Nehemiah, however, were convinced that the Gentiles were a danger to the purity of Israel's faith. They wanted to establish a clear division between Jew and Gentile. The fact that Gentiles were forbidden from entering certain sections of the temple in Jerusalem is a further indication of the partition that existed between the two. How would this traditional separation influence the mission of the church? In this section of Acts, Luke attempted to show how the church dealt with the issue of a mission to the Gentiles.

Peter, Cornelius and the Mission to the Gentiles (9:32—12:25)

This is a very lengthy and a very important section in Acts. Like the other sections covered in this chapter, it deserves much more comment that we are able to give it here.

In the opening part of this section (9:32—11:18) Luke included three incidents that involved Peter. Each of them is similar to an event in Jesus' ministry and each of them is somewhat like occurrences in Paul's ministry, described later in Acts.

The first incident was the healing of Aeneas who had been a paralytic and bedridden for eight years. Lydda, where Aeneas lived, was a few miles south of the coastal town of Joppa. While Peter was visiting the Christians ("saints") at Lydda, he met Aeneas and served as the instrument for his healing. As a consequence of the miracle done to Aeneas, a large number of people in the town and nearby became Christians. Compare this story with Jesus' ministry in Luke 5:18–26 and Paul's work in Acts 14:8–12.

In the second incident Peter was summoned to Joppa from Lydda by Christian disciples who were mourning the death of one of their number, a woman named Tabitha whose Greek name was Dorcas, which meant gazelle. Tabitha was an outstanding member of the Christian community, a person "full of good works and acts of charity." After his arrival in Joppa, Peter went to the home where Tabitha's body had been laid. He asked the mourners to leave the room while he knelt in prayer. When he spoke to Tabitha's body saying, "Tabitha, rise," her life returned and Peter called for the disciples to witness this amazing event. When the restoration of Tabitha's life became known in Joppa, many people became followers of Jesus. This story is comparable to Jesus' deeds in Luke 8:49–56 and Paul's ministry in Acts 20:7–12.

The third incident involving Peter is one of the most important episodes in Acts. It describes Peter's ministry to

Cornelius, the Roman military officer and the first Gentile to embrace the Christian faith and to become a member of the church.

Cornelius was a resident of Caesarea, a seaport on the Mediterranean Sea and the administrative capital of the Roman government in Palestine. He was the commander of one hundred soldiers. Hence, the term "centurion." He belonged to the Italian Cohort. A cohort might be composed of up to six hundred men, one-tenth the size of a Roman legion. While Cornelius was not a Jew, he was a "God-fearer," someone who worshipped God and probably attended the synagogue. He gave liberally to the poor and prayed regularly. Cornelius was a Gentile. He had not completely accepted the Jewish religion nor had he been circumcised.

Through a vision God told Cornelius that he should send representatives to Joppa to invite Peter to visit him in Caesarea. He immediately dispatched three messengers to do as God had ordered.

As Cornelius' men were on their way to find Peter in Joppa, Peter had a vision of his own. While he was in prayer and while his friends were preparing a meal for him, he fell into a trance and had a dream. He saw something like a large sheet of cloth descending from heaven on which were various animals, reptiles and birds. He also heard a voice that told him to kill these creatures and to eat them. Peter protested that these creatures were unfit for eating according to the Jewish food laws (Leviticus 11). But the voice replied that Peter should not consider them common and unclean. ("What God has cleansed, you must not call common" 9:15.)

When he awoke from his dream Peter wondered about its meaning. As he pondered the matter the three messengers of Cornelius arrived at the place where he was staying. Moved by the Spirit, Peter spoke with them and agreed to accompany them to Cornelius' home in Caesarea. We can imagine some of Peter's misgivings as he traveled to Cornelius' home. Even if Cornelius were a "God-fearer," he was still a Gentile and a Roman military officer. What could he possibly want from Peter?

Peter must have been surprised when he arrived at Cornelius' residence. Not only did he find the centurion anxiously awaiting his visit, but he also discovered that

Cornelius had gathered his family and close friends in anticipation of Peter's appearance. Furthermore, Cornelius knelt at Peter's feet as a sign of respect for the apostle. Peter refused this unusual expression of homage (compare this with Paul's experiences in 14:8–18 and 28:6) and began to converse with Cornelius. He indicated that although the Jewish law made it difficult for free associations with Gentiles and visits to their homes, he had been shown in a vision that *no one* created by God should be shunned as common or unclean. Cornelius proceeded to recount the story of his vision in which he was directed to send for Peter in order to hear what message God would speak through him.

The stage had been set by Luke for another major speech in Acts. It was the first recorded sermon to a Gentile audience. Peter stated his conviction that God showed no nationalistic partiality. All were accepted who did God's will. He proclaimed that Jesus, anointed with God's Spirit and power, was the Lord and Judge of all through whom everyone may receive the forgiveness of sins. Even as Peter spoke, something amazing happened. The Holy Spirit, God's presence and power, came upon the Gentile audience and they began to praise God in ecstatic speech. Peter ordered that these Gentiles be baptized, thereby recognizing their full incorporation into the church. They asked him to remain with them for several days, perhaps so that he might provide additional instruction for them concerning the Way. Another major barrier had been broken by the gospel. Now Gentiles as well as Jews and Samaritans had become members of the Christian community.

News about the Gentiles becoming followers of Jesus reached the rest of the apostles and disciples in Judea. When Peter returned to Jerusalem, some of them who were known as the "circumcision party," or strict Jewish Christians, were critical of Peter for associating with Gentiles. This gave Peter the opportunity to tell them about his vision in Joppa and Cornelius' vision in Caesarea. He also reported how the Holy Spirit was given to the Gentiles just as the Spirit had been received in Jerusalem on Pentecost. Peter ended his address by saying, "If then God gave the same gift to them as he gave to us when we believed in the Lord Jesus Christ, who was I that I could withstand God?" Those who had been critical of Peter's work among the Gentiles were silenced. They recognized that

God's grace had been extended to the Gentiles just as it had been granted to them.

Luke continued to describe the progress of the Christian message among the Gentiles. He stated that some of the disciples had great success in preaching to the Gentiles in Antioch, the capital of the Roman province of Syria. The church in Jerusalem, which retained its place as the most prominent group among the earliest Christians, sent Barnabas to inspect the work in Antioch. Barnabas was delighted with what he observed. He sent to Tarsus for Saul, and for the next year Barnabas and Saul nurtured the followers of Jesus in Antioch. It was in Antioch, Luke claimed, that the disciples were first called "Christians," a term found only three times in the New Testament (Acts 11:26; 26:28; I Peter 4:16).

The bond that existed between Jewish and Gentile Christians was evident in their concern for one another and in their sharing of material goods. This practice was a continuation of the voluntary sharing that had characterized the Christian community from its origin. When Agabus, moved by the Spirit, foresaw a worldwide famine, the Gentile disciples in Antioch resolved to share whatever they had with their sisters and brothers in Judea (11:27-30). This was the most concrete way of expressing their solidarity and fellowship with those who shared their faith. They used their wealth to meet needs and to undergird their community of faith.

Regrettably, the persecution of Christians persisted under the leadership of King Herod Agrippa I (12:1) who ruled Palestine A.D. 41 to 44. Herod murdered James the brother of John (12:2), the first of the twelve apostles to be martyred. Since this act pleased some of those who opposed the church, Herod proceeded to arrest Peter and to have him imprisoned. As in an earlier episode (5:17-21), however, Peter was mysteriously delivered from his confinement. At first, Peter himself could not believe that God was liberating him from captivity (12:9). But his disbelief soon changed to a realization that God had actually rescued him (12:11).

Following his escape from prison, Peter went to the home of Mary, the mother of John Mark, where some of the disciples were meeting. When the servant answered Peter's knock at the door and recognized his voice, she was so overjoyed that she left him standing outside and ran to tell the others that Peter was there. They did not believe her. Peter continued to knock at the door until those inside opened it, saw him, and were astonished by his story about God's deliverance. Peter instructed them to tell the tale of his captivity and release to James the brother of Jesus, who was one of the most important leaders of the early church, and to the rest of the community. Peter then left for a place where he would be safe from Herod. Herod was so angered by Peter's escape from prison that he ordered the prison sentries killed.

Luke also included in this section of Acts a brief account of Herod's death (12:20–23). Herod for some reason became angry with the people of the Phoenician cities of Tyre and Sidon. When they attempted to appease him, he accepted their flattery and their idolatrous designation that he was a god. Immediately, Luke reported, Herod was stricken by God and died.

The church grew stronger. It had not only been able to resolve internal problems, but was able to overcome its opposition, even the violent threats of a tyrant like Herod. Barnabas and Saul returned to Antioch from Jerusalem with a new companion, John Mark, and were prepared for the next phase of the church's mission.

Paul's First Missionary Journey and the Council at Jerusalem (13:1—15:35)

In the church at Antioch were leaders, both men and women, known as prophets and teachers. The duty of the prophets and teachers was to serve as a means by which God's word was conveyed to the human community. They were also responsible for interpreting the life and teaching of Jesus in light of what the Old Testament scriptures said about the promised Anointed One of God (the Messiah, the Christ). It was believed that prophets and teachers received gifts from the Holy Spirit that enabled them to perform their work.

Barnabas, Symeon, Lucius, Manaen and Saul are named in Acts 13:1 as among those who had received the necessary gifts to occupy positions as prophets and teachers. As they were engaged in worship and fasting (abstention from food), perhaps with the rest of the church in Antioch, the Spirit moved them to set apart Barnabas and Saul for special work. These two men were commissioned, blessed and invested with authority to act on behalf of the Christians at Antioch through the laying on of hands. After this ceremony, Barnabas and Saul set off on what Luke described as the first of Saul's (Paul's) three missionary journeys.

Luke emphasized God's role in this first missionary trip by saying that Barnabas and Saul were sent out by the Holy Spirit. They also had a companion, John Mark, who assisted them. The three men sailed to Cyprus, an island in the eastern Mediterranean about sixty miles west of the coast of Syria. They went to Salamis, the chief town of Cyprus, and began their mission work in the synagogue. The synagogue was a building in which an assembly of Jewish people met for prayer, to listen to the reading of scripture, and to hear preaching and teaching based on the scriptures. To this day it retains major significance for the religious life of Judaism. The synagogue was a natural place for Barnabas and Saul to initiate their mission work in many of the cities and towns they visited since they were convinced that the message about Jesus had to be proclaimed first to their fellow Jews.

After their visit to Salamis, Saul and Barnabas traveled across Cyprus to Paphos, the capital city of the island on its southwestern coast. In Paphos they encountered a magician named Bar-Jesus who was also known as Elymas. As we noted earlier, the early Christians were very skeptical about the use of magic and those associated with it. Remember the story of Simon the magician in 8:9–24. In addition to being a magician, Elymas was also branded a "false prophet" by Luke, that is, one who falsely claimed that he conveyed God's message in his words and deeds.

Apparently, Saul and Barnabas were impressing Sergius Paulus, the Roman official who governed Cyprus, with their preaching and teaching. Elymas was disturbed by their success and tried to interfere with their work. Saul denounced Elymas and claimed that God would cause the magician to be struck blind. When blindness did fall on Elymas, Sergius Paulus was astonished and began to believe in the divine power at work in the ministry of Saul and Barnabas. The point of this incident is to convince the readers of Acts that magic and the false prophet are no match for the power of God.

It is important to note that beginning with 13:9 and

throughout the remainder of Acts, except for two speeches which refer to his conversion experience, Saul is called Paul, the Roman form of his name. Nowhere in the New Testament except in Acts is it recorded that Paul, a Hellenistic Jew and a Roman citizen, was ever called by the Jewish name, Saul.

Luke did not give any further details about Paul's work in Paphos nor did he say how long it lasted. This type of information is lacking in many of the incidents described in Acts, especially those related to Paul's missionary journeys. As a result, it is very easy for the reader to overlook such basic issues as the hardships, hazards, and time involved in traveling from place to place in Paul's day.

Paul and his companions traveled next to Perga in Pamphylia, about twelve miles inland from the southern coast of Asia Minor, and then on to Antioch, a mountainous town in Pisidia located to the north of Pamphylia. In Pisidian Antioch, not to be confused with Syrian Antioch, Paul and Barnabas entered the synagogue. After the scriptures were read they were invited to speak to the assembly. On this occasion Paul delivered an address in which he presented a brief summary of Israel's history. He stated that Israel had been chosen by God and given its promised land. God had raised up rulers among the people of Israel. Finally, God had given them a Savior, Jesus. Although Jesus had been killed, God had raised him from the dead. Through Jesus God was proclaiming that the forgiveness of everyone's sins was possible.

When Paul finished his address, many asked him to return to the synagogue on the following sabbath to continue his instruction. When the next sabbath arrived, a very large crowd gathered to hear Paul. Some of those present, however, disrupted the meeting and spoke out strongly against him. Paul and Barnabas were upset by the angry opposition to their message. They stated their intention from that point on to take the message about Jesus to the Gentiles (13:46; compare with 18:5-6). Luke claimed that the Gentiles in the area gladly received the message Paul and Barnabas preached. Those who opposed them were successful in driving them out of the area; however, the new disciples who were left behind were full of joy and the presence of the Holy Spirit.

Paul and Barnabas traveled east from Pisidian Antioch to Iconium, a city in south-central Asia Minor. Although they had said that they intended to take their message to the Gentiles, their first recorded stop in Iconium was the Jewish synagogue where they addressed both Jews and some Gentiles who were evidently sympathetic to Judaism. Some of those present became Christians. Again, others, in spite of the "signs and wonders" done by Paul and Barnabas, succeeded in forcing them to flee for their lives to Lystra, a Roman colony about twenty-five miles southwest of Iconium.

At Lystra, Paul and Barnabas found a man who had been crippled from birth. In an incident similar to the healing of the crippled man at the temple gate in Jerusalem (3:1–10), this lame man was also healed. Those who witnessed the incident praised Paul and Barnabas as gods. They referred to Barnabas as Zeus, the chief of the Greek gods, and they gave Paul the name of Hermes, the messenger and orator of the Greek gods. Horrified by this tribute, Paul and Barnabas claimed that they were merely human beings, not gods, who had come to tell the people of Lystra about the living God who had created all beings and who had blessed them "with food and gladness."

In the meantime, those from Pisidian Antioch and Iconium, who had already created problems for Paul and Barnabas, pursued them to Lystra. With apparent ease they persuaded the people of Lystra that the two Christian preachers were worthy only to be killed. A mob attacked Paul and almost stoned him to death. Surprisingly, Paul recovered quickly from the assault and was able to accompany Barnabas to Derbe, a town in central Asia Minor a short distance from Lystra. In Derbe they were successful in helping a number of persons become disciples of Christ.

There are at least two outstanding features of the next section of the book (14:21–23). First, Paul and Barnabas decided to return to Syrian Antioch, the city from which they had begun their first missionary journey. Incredibly, they chose to return by way of the cities where they had encountered stiff opposition and violence—Lystra, Iconium and Pisidian Antioch. They disregarded the danger that seemingly awaited them in those places for the sake of visiting those who had become disciples under their ministry. For them the gospel was not a call to safety, but to risk.

Second, the purpose of their visit was to nurture their sisters and brothers in Christ. They exhorted them to remain faithful and prayed for them. They assured them that in spite of difficult times, which were inevitable for the new disciples, they would be sustained by God's presence. Finally, they appointed leaders in every church who would supervise the worship, instruction, discipline and administration of each congregation. Paul and Barnabas understood that nurture was crucial. If the new Christians were not encouraged to grow, their faith would likely dwindle and their witness would become barren.

The first missionary journey ended with stops in Perga and Attalia before Paul and Barnabas sailed for Antioch in Syria. When they arrived in Antioch they assembled the church and declared how God had worked with them and how God "had opened a door of faith to the Gentiles."

There were some Christians from Judea who were skeptical about whether Gentiles could be genuine Christians if they did not observe the customs of the Jewish law including circumcision. They argued this matter with Paul and Barnabas and for a time it appeared that the Christian movement might split into two separate segments—Jewish Christians and Gentile Christians. Paul and Barnabas were sent to Jerusalem to meet with the apostles and other leaders in order to resolve the question of requiring Gentile Christians to be circumcised and to comply with the Jewish law. The important meeting where these issues were discussed is often referred to as the Jerusalem Council. It was a very critical event in the early history of the church, although there are significant differences between Luke and Paul (Galatians 2:1–10) regarding the council and its results.

The assembled leaders heard a speech by Peter who celebrated God's work among the Gentiles and warned that the Gentile Christians must not be burdened with legalism. Peter's speech at the Jerusalem Council marks his last appearance in Acts. The assembly also listened as Paul and Barnabas told of God's accomplishments through them among the Gentiles. Finally, James, presumably the brother of Jesus, addressed the council. He, too, spoke with approval about the Gentiles being included among God's people and quoted Amos 9:11–12 to support his view (Acts 15:16–18). James called on the assembly to set aside the requirement that Gentile Christians be circumcised, but he asked that they be obligated to abstain from three things prohibited under the Jewish law: (1) food that had originally been used for sacrificial purposes in pagan religious ceremonies; (2) illicit sexual intercourse; (3) eating the meat of animals that had been strangled, meat not properly drained of its blood (Leviticus 17:8–14).

James' leadership in the early church is evident in this episode of the Jerusalem Council. The assembly accepted his plan and sent Paul, Barnabas, Judas Barsabbas and Silas (15:22) with a letter for the Gentile Christians containing James' proposal. According to Luke, when the Gentiles at Antioch received the letter they were very pleased and expressed their willingness to abide by its provisions. The church would not be divided. Jew and Gentile would be one in Christ.

Paul's Mission Work Continues To Receive Mixed Reviews (15:36—19:20)

Since the Jerusalem Council had settled the argument about the Gentiles and the Jewish law, Paul and Barnabas prepared to set out on a second missionary journey (15:36—18:22), the major purpose of which was to return to some of the cities where they had begun churches. Before they started, however, they quarreled about whether John Mark should accompany them. He had abandoned them on their earlier trip (13:13). As a result of their dispute, Paul and Barnabas separated. This incident marked the last mention of Barnabas in Acts. From this point on, Luke turned his attention exclusively to the mission work of Paul.

Paul chose Silas to accompany him (15:40) and traveled through Syria and Cilicia to Derbe and Lystra. At Lystra he met and circumcised Timothy, who became a trusted friend and companion. Timothy's circumcision seems strange in light of the Jerusalem Council's decision, but since Timothy was of partial Jewish ancestry, Paul could have felt his circumcision would ease his ministry among those of Jewish background.

Luke again emphasized the guidance of the Holy Spirit in Paul's work. The Spirit prevented him from preaching in Asia (16:6) and from going into Bithynia, a Roman province in northwest Asia Minor. In a vision, however, Paul was instructed to travel to Macedonia (Greece) where he entered Europe for the first time. Note in 16:10 the first use of the pronoun "we," which gives the impression that the author of Acts himself was present on this and other phases of Paul's travels. However, some scholars suggest that this may imply the inclusion of diary material by someone else other than Luke.

When Paul reached the Macedonian city of Philippi, he decided to spend several days there. Luke described three incidents related to Paul's stay. First, Paul met with a group of women, one of whom was Lydia, a wealthy merchant who sold luxurious purple-dyed cloth. After listening to Paul she became a disciple, was baptized with her household, and offered hospitality to Paul and his associates (16:12–15).

In the second incident (16:16–24), Paul encountered a slave girl whose owners claimed that she could secure information about matters and events hidden to most people. Her owners profited by her powers of divination. When Paul expelled the evil force in the slave girl, her owners were so angry that they had Paul and Silas seized, beaten and thrown into prison. One commentator has said of this event:

> It is a Lukan belief that vested financial interests, when threatened, oppose the gospel. This fact is foreshadowed in Luke 8:37 where the Gerasenes ask Jesus to leave their country because the healing of the demoniac cost them financially. This emphasis will crop up again in Acts 19:23-41 when in Ephesus, the business of those who make silver shrines of Artemis is threatened by the gospel. The economic motivation of those opposed to the Christian missionaries [in the story of the slave girl] is masked behind various other appeals: Paul and Silas are branded as foreigners (an appeal to nationalistic feeling); they are labeled Jews (an appeal to racial prejudice); they are described as purveyors of new ideas (an appeal to traditionalism); and they are depicted as opposed to Rome (an appeal to patriotism).[1]

The third incident occurred while Paul and Silas were bound and held in a Philippian prison (16:25–34). An earthquake, undoubtedly viewed as divine intervention, dislodged the locked doors and shackles that held the prisoners. Believing that his prisoners had escaped, the warden, who was held responsible, was ready to kill himself. But Paul and his fellow prisoners had not left. As a consequence, the jailer became a disciple, was baptized with his family, and invited Paul and Silas to his home. A short time later the authorities ordered that

Paul and Silas be officially freed, but Paul would not go until the magistrates came and apologized to him.

It is interesting that in these three incidents the ministry of the church crossed traditional economic lines. Lydia represented wealth. The slave girl was a poor, exploited person. The Philippian jailer was probably neither rich nor poor. Yet, all three were recipients of the church's ministry through Paul.

Paul and Silas moved on to Thessalonica and Beroea, two Macedonian cities west of Philippi (17:1–13). They visited the synagogues in both cities and received the usual mixed responses. Some accepted their message and became disciples. Others opposed their work and sought to harm them. When the situation in Beroea became tense, his friends persuaded Paul to move on to Athens.

In Paul's time, Athens was not the great city it had been when Greece ruled the ancient world, but it was still an important cultural and intellectual center. Paul was not content to take his message only to the synagogue in Athens, but also presented it in the "market place," the center of the city's social, political and commercial life. He was upset by the evidences of idolatry he found throughout the city. Epicureans, who were generally uninterested in believing in any god, and Stoics, who held that the universe was held together and animated by a divine purpose or reason, were among the wide variety of people with whom Paul conversed in the city. Some were fascinated by his message about Jesus and the resurrection because it was something new to them. Luke added, somewhat sarcastically, "Now all the Athenians and the foreigners who lived there spent their time in nothing except telling or hearing something new" (17:21).

Paul was taken to the Areopagus, a low hill in Athens near the famous acropolis, where he was asked to address a crowd of those interested in his views. He used the occasion to attack idolatry and to proclaim the one God who created all things and who demanded repentance from all people. The Paul portrayed by Luke asserted that God had fixed a day on which the world would be judged by the risen Christ who had been appointed by God for that task. Some mocked. Others were curious to hear more. Still others believed, including a man named Dionysius the Areopagite and a woman named Damaris.

When Paul considered his work in Athens to be complete, he

moved on to Corinth, one of the major commercial cities of the time. In Corinth Paul met Priscilla and Aquila who were apparently already Christians. Paul was able to lodge with them since they all practiced the same trade. They were tentmakers or leatherworkers.

Paul attended the synagogue in Corinth on the sabbath and was successful in persuading some of those present to become Christians. However, after Silas and Timothy joined him in Corinth, substantial opposition began to appear. Similar to his reaction to the opposition in Pisidian Antioch (13:46), Paul announced his intention to take his appeal for discipleship to the Gentiles. Nevertheless, one of the leading persons in the synagogue and his family became followers of the Way. Other Corinthians also accepted Paul's message and were baptized.

Paul and his companions continued to preach and teach in Corinth for eighteen months. During that time they were assured by God that they must speak boldly and that they would not be harmed. Paul's opponents brought charges against him before Gallio, the governor of the province. They alleged that Paul's teaching was not in keeping with the Jewish law. Before Paul had an opportunity to defend himself, however, Gallio dismissed the charges and had Paul's accusers driven from his presence. Then some members of Gallio's court apparently seized Sosthenes, the leader of the opposition to Paul, and beat him as a sign of their disdain for the group he represented.

Sometime later Paul decided to return to Antioch in Syria. Before he left Greece with Priscilla and Aquila, Luke tells us he stopped at Cenchreae and completed a vow he had made. Such a vow usually involved a pledge to abstain from alcoholic beverages and was concluded by the cutting of one's hair. (See Numbers 6:5, 18–20.)

On their way to Antioch, Paul and his friends stopped in Ephesus and Caesarea. His arrival in Antioch (18:22) marked the end of what is commonly known as his second missionary journey. After a time in Antioch, Paul was ready to undertake what has come to be known as his third missionary trip (18:23—21:16). His route took him through Cilicia, Galatia and Phrygia toward Ephesus.

Before Luke described Paul's work in Ephesus, however, he introduced another personality in the early church named Apollos. Apollos was a native of Alexandria, a renowned center of culture and education in Egypt. Apollos had not only been influenced by the rich intellectual environment of Alexandria, but was also well grounded in knowledge of the Hebrew scriptures. Furthermore, Apollos had become a Christian and had taught others about Jesus even "though he knew only the baptism of John," the Baptist (18:25). After Priscilla and Aquila heard Apollos speak, they taught him even more about the Way. He was an important leader in the early church (I Corinthians 1:12 and 3:4–6).

When Paul finally arrived at Ephesus, he discovered there about a dozen people who knew nothing of the Holy Spirit but who had been baptized into the way of John the Baptist. They submitted to being baptized again (19:5) in the name of Jesus and, through the laying on of hands, received the Holy Spirit and the gift of inspired speech. Paul continued to preach and to show concern for the sick. He visited the synagogue where he spoke about the kingdom of God. When he met with opposition there, he carried on his ministry in the lecture hall of Tyrannus in the city. In addition, unusual healings took place by his hands.

There were seven sons of a Jewish religious leader named Sceva who attempted to expel evil spirits and heal people as Paul did. They even invoked the name of Jesus in their work. However, their attempt to perform these deeds and to use the power of God for their own benefit failed. Luke closed this section by observing again that compared to the gospel, magic was useless, if not dangerous. Like Simon the magician (8:9–24) and Elymas (13:6–12), those who practiced magic in Ephesus found that it was worthless and they destroyed their handbooks of magical incantations and formulas.

Paul's Determination to Return to Jerusalem Vested Interests in Ephesus (19:21—21:16)

After about two years, Paul's work in Ephesus drew to a close and the Spirit prompted him to consider travel through Greece (Macedonia and Achaia) in order to return to Jerusalem. From there he would then make a trip to Rome. While still in Ephesus, he sent two of his helpers, Timothy and Erastus, into Greece to prepare the way for his visit.

Before Paul could leave Ephesus a major conflict developed

between the Christian community and the silversmiths of the town. Ephesus was not only an important port city in western Asia Minor, it was also the location of a large temple, one of the seven wonders of the ancient world, and a number of smaller silver shrines built to honor Artemis, the Ephesian goddess of nature and fertility. The presence of the temple and the silver shrines (miniature temples) provided a brisk and prosperous business for the local silversmiths. Through one of their leaders, a man named Demetrius, these craftsmen voiced their complaints about Paul's message that gods made of silver by human hands were not gods at all. The gospel preached by Paul was a threat to their trade and to the tourist business attracted to Ephesus by Artemis's temple and silver shrines.

At the instigation of Demetrius and his enraged associates, there was a great turmoil in the city and two of Paul's companions were seized by a mob and dragged through the streets. Paul wanted to address the mob, but his friends, including some Asiarchs (Roman administrative officials), begged him not to appear before the crowd, which appeared to be confused about the whole affair. A Jew named Alexander attempted to address the mob, perhaps to inform them that his people were not associated with the Christians. The crowd would not listen to him. A leading official in the city, however, was able to quiet the mob. He stated that the Christians who had been seized were no threat to the worship of Artemis and that any charges against them should be dealt with through the regular legal system. If the unruly crowd did not disband, he asserted, they could be charged with rioting and unpleasant consequences might follow. Persuaded by the official's appeal, the crowd dispersed. As in the case of the slave girl and her owner (16:16–24), the gospel had come into conflict with vested financial interests, which were unable to overcome it.

When the disorder in Ephesus stopped, Paul left the city and traveled to Greece where he spent three months. He then retraced his steps to Troas, an important seaport on the northwest coast of Asia Minor. While in Troas, Paul held a meeting with some of the disciples that went late into the night. One of them, a young man named Eutychus, became sleepy during the meeting and fell from the third-story window in which he was sitting. According to Luke, Eutychus "was taken up dead," but Paul embraced his lifeless body, saying "his life is in him." So Eutychus was restored to life and ate and conversed with those present.

Paul resumed his journey toward Jerusalem with several stops including an important visit in Miletus, a large port and commercial center on the west coast of Asia Minor. When he arrived in Miletus, Paul sent for the leaders of the church at Ephesus and addressed them in a lengthy speech (20:18–35). It was his final opportunity to speak to them before he set out for Jerusalem.

Paul's speech contains what we would expect from a farewell address. He spoke about his accomplishments, his faithfulness, and the suffering the Holy Spirit revealed in his future. Paul exhorted these leaders to follow his example by nurturing the church, being alert to the dangers that might threaten it, and avoiding any greediness for personal gain that might be a temptation. He concluded his speech with words from Jesus not recorded anywhere else in the New Testament, "It is more blessed to give than to receive." The lasting impression of Paul's speech is that the exemplary actions of a Christian leader set a pattern for, and may be an inspiration to, the rest of the Christian community.

As a final act of fellowship, Paul prayed with his sisters and brothers in Christ at Miletus. They wept, knowing that they would not see him again. Paul and his companions then set sail again. They stopped at Tyre and at Caesarea where Paul's friends warned him that trouble awaited him at Jerusalem. At Caesarea, the prophet Agabus, who a few years earlier had warned of a world famine (11:27–30) cautioned Paul that his trip to Jerusalem was extremely dangerous. Paul's reply was, ". . . I am ready not only to be imprisoned but even to die at Jerusalem for the name of the Lord Jesus." Like his Lord, Paul felt compelled by the Spirit to go to Jerusalem no matter what the consequences. As he neared Jerusalem, his third missionary journey came to an end.

Acts for Our Time

We have covered a vast amount of material in this section of Acts. The episodes Luke described for us are very useful in thinking about our situation as faithful and thoughtful Christian disciples today. A few themes stand out.

First, one of the questions that may be raised as we study Acts, and especially the section we have just completed, is its image of Judaism. Repeatedly in the book Luke appears to speak critically and negatively about the Jews. Some may conclude that he was, therefore, expressing anti-semitic views and laying a biblical base for the monstrous, ghastly and ungodly acts Christians have committed against Jews over the ensuing centuries. But was Luke anti-semitic?

Luke himself may have been a Jew. Even if he were not Jewish, it is evident that he possessed a very high regard for Jewish history and the Hebrew scriptures cited frequently in the speeches of apostles and disciples in Acts. Furthermore, he clearly showed that the earliest Christians and their leaders, such as Peter, James and Paul, were Jews who greatly valued their religious heritage and recognized that God's acts in the life, death and resurrection of Jesus were rooted in the foundations of God's acts in the history of Israel. While Luke spoke negatively about Jews at certain places in Acts, it was his way of identifying a certain group whose views were opposed to Christian teachings and who actively engaged in trying to destroy the Christian movement. There is no justification for anti-semitism in Acts.

Second, this section of the book reminds us that there are forces in the world opposed to the love, power and justice of God. Unlike Jonah who walked unopposed through Nineveh, proclaiming God's message, the early Christians encountered stiff resistance from those whose traditionalism blinded them to new ways of seeing and experiencing God's renewing presence and grace. Moreover, the early disciples were forced to endure the antagonism of those whose vested financial interests were threatened by the Way. We can always expect the forces of evil to defy and to contend against the reign of God. One of the important lessons of the crucifixion and resurrection echoed in Acts is that while the comfort of the Christian is never guaranteed, the success of the mission is ultimately assured.

Third, Acts testifies that even the most difficult circumstances provide the Christian with opportunities to be a witness for the truth. Repeatedly in Acts, the seizures, beatings and imprisonments of the disciples became occasions for them to experience God's sustaining grace and to demonstrate their commitment to God's rule in the world. Paul's arrest and imprisonment in Philippi as a result of his liberating the slave girl (16:16–34) recalls the lives of other disciples who have been jailed for their testimony to God's purpose.

Martin Luther King, Jr. used his imprisonment in Birmingham in April, 1963, to prick the conscience of Americans and his fellow Christians. His "Letter From Birmingham Jail" was a clear call for an end to racism and injustice. In that letter, King answered those who criticized his role as a "trouble–maker" by alluding to the book of Acts:

> Whenever the early Christians entered a town, the people in power became disturbed and immediately sought to convict the Christians for being "disturbers of the peace" and "outside agitators." But the Christians pressed on in the conviction that they were a "colony of heaven," and called to obey God rather than man. Small in number, they were big in commitment. They were too God-intoxicated to be [numerically] intimidated.[2]

At this very moment there are Christians in this world who are in prison or otherwise suffering because of their faith. They are enduring by the grace of God as they refuse to be anything less than faithful witnesses. They need our prayers and whatever comfort and support we may offer them.

A fourth theme in this section of Acts is the importance of nurture in the Christian community. From the beginning the early Christians recognized that fellowship, worship and learning were indispensable if they were to fulfill Jesus' commission, which was both a gift and a task. So we have read about Paul's returning to strengthen the churches begun under his ministry. Priscilla and Aquila enabled Apollos to become a more effective servant of God through their instruction. Those early Christians drew strength from one another. They learned from one another. They were inspired as they worshipped together. Growth in Christ is not an option. Furthermore, it does not usually occur accidentally. Christian nurture is critical for deepening our faith and broadening our witness.

Questions and Suggestions

1. How is Christianity related to Judaism? What do they have in common? How can Christians better understand Judaism and combat the anti-semitism often evident in what they say and do?

2. Why did Paul say on at least two occasions (Acts 13:46; 18:6) that he was going to turn his attention to the Gentiles, but then continue to work in Jewish synagogues?

3. The main question at the Jerusalem Council was whether Gentile Christians would be required to observe the customs and practices of Judaism including circumcision. This issue had to do with what was central to Christian faith and what was peripheral to it. Are there any areas today where one group of Christians expects another group to comply with a custom or practice not really central or necessary to the faith?

4. The early Christians encountered fierce opposition in Ephesus when they threatened vested financial interests. What are some present financial interests that might find the gospel a menace? In what ways do the defenders of these interests seek to intimidate their critics?

5. While Paul was in Troas, Luke reported that on the first day of the week (Sunday) he broke bread with the Christians who gathered there (20:7). Although some claim that this was a celebration of the Lord's Supper, others say the text is not clear on this point. The Lord's Supper seems relatively unimportant in Acts. The book of Acts reflects an early Christian community living in the expectation of Jesus' return in the near future. This being the case, probably the Lord's supper as a sacrament had not yet been incorporated into the community's practices. Perhaps you could research the origins and the meaning of the Lord's Supper and how it is connected with who we are and what the church is and does.

6. What is the responsibility of the Christian and the Christian community to our brothers and sisters who have been arrested and perhaps even imprisoned for the sake of a matter of conscience?

7. In preparation for the next session of the group read Acts 21:17—28:31.

CHAPTER VI

To the End of the Earth
ACTS 21:17—28:31

The last eight chapters of Acts deal with the continuing work of Paul. They describe the various schemes by those who were opposed to his ministry, his confrontations with religious and governmental leaders, and his harrowing journey to Rome. These sections of the book comprise Luke's way of telling the final part of the story of how Jesus' witnesses carried their message from Jerusalem to the end of the earth, from a city the Romans considered remote and insignificant to the city that was the capital of their empire.

Trouble in Jerusalem (21:17—23:11)

When Paul arrived in Jerusalem he was met by a number of Christian disciples who greeted him warmly. He met with James the brother of Jesus and other leaders of the church. There is no mention of the apostles here or anywhere else in the rest of the book. Paul narrated for James and the elders at Jerusalem the amazing results of God's acts among the Gentiles through his ministry. They were delighted to hear his report and gave thanks to God for it. One of their number then addressed him on behalf of the whole group.

Paul was informed that a large number of Jewish Christians were very suspicious of his work among the Gentiles. It had been alleged that Paul had told the Gentiles to ignore the Jewish religious laws and customs and not to circumcise their children. (Note his letter to the Galatians in this respect.)

Somehow, the leaders stated, Paul was to demonstrate that these allegations were false. He was to prove that he was loyal to the law. How? He could join four of the Jewish Christian disciples who had taken the Nazirite vow and were about ready to shave their heads as a sign of thanksgiving and loyalty to God (see Numbers 6:1–21 for more information on the vow). Furthermore, Paul could pay all of the expenses incurred by the four who took the vow including the cost of the appropriate sacrifices in the temple at the end of the vow. This would be a sign that Paul still respected the law and customs of Judaism. At the close of the 'brethren's' speech the provisions of the decree of the Jerusalem Council were repeated (Acts 21:25; compare with 15:20; 15:29). Acts implies that without dissent Paul complied. He joined the men who had taken the vow, purified himself of ritual uncleanness, and paid the expenses as he had been requested. Luke included this story undoubtedly as a sign of Paul's willingness to maintain harmony in the Christian community.

Near the end of the period of his vow, Paul was spotted in the temple by some of his opponents from Asia. They incited a crowd to anger against Paul by making the same accusations against him as those that had been lodged against Stephen (6:13). They charged that everywhere he went Paul attacked the law and the temple. In addition, they stated, he had defiled the temple by bringing a Gentile into that part of the temple forbidden to those who were not Jews. The crowd grew larger and became violent. They seized Paul, dragged him from the temple and attempted to beat him to death.

When news of the disturbance reached Claudius Lysias, the commander of the Roman garrison responsible for keeping order in the temple area, he led some of his soldiers to the place of the commotion. He placed Paul under arrest and ordered him bound in chains. There was such great confusion at the place of Paul's arrest that the commander had to have Paul carried through the crowd. The mob angrily shouted for Paul's death in a manner similar to the crowd's reaction at the time of Jesus' trial (Luke 23:18–23).

Before Paul and the soldiers reached the Roman barracks, the commander asked him if he was the Egyptian who had recently led a group of violent nationalists, called Assassins, in a revolt against Roman rule, near Jerusalem. Paul replied that he was not the Egyptian, but a Jew from Tarsus, the capital of Cilicia. Then Paul made a surprising request. He asked the commander if he would permit him to address the angry crowd. When the commander gave his approval, Paul, standing on the barracks steps, spoke to the crowd in their own language. Hearing Paul address them in Hebrew (or Aramaic) prompted the crowd to be more attentive to his words.

Luke then recorded Paul's lengthy apologetic speech in which he defended his ministry. It was in the form of an autobiographical statement. The speech is divided into four main parts. The first section (22:1, 3–5) emphasized his relationship to Judaism. He stated that he was a Jew by birth, devoted to the law, educated by the revered Pharisee, Gamaliel, and a fierce persecutor of the Christians. This is the only mention in Acts that Paul received instruction from Gamaliel, whose speech to the Sanhedrin earlier in Acts (5:33–39) probably saved the lives of Peter and the apostles. It must be noted that Gamaliel is never mentioned in any of Paul's letters, even when Paul emphasized his own Pharasaic background. In the second section of Paul's speech (22:6–11) he told about his mysterious experience of the risen Christ on the road to Damascus. The third section (22:12–16) recounted the role of Ananias as the bearer of God's commissioning of Paul as a witness for Christ. The final section (22:17–21) underscored the change God had made in Paul's life and spoke of God's call for him to preach to the Gentiles.

Paul's speech did not create calm among the crowd. Rather, it provoked them to such fury that the commander had to take Paul into the barracks in order to protect him. Once inside, however, the commander ordered that Paul be scourged, that is, whipped with leather thongs laced with sharp pieces of bone and lead. Perhaps the commander thought such a beating would induce Paul to reveal facts he had up to this point withheld. When the prisoner had been prepared for the scourging, he stunned the commander by claiming that he was born a Roman citizen and, therefore, could not be whipped without having been sentenced by the proper Roman authorities. Unfortunately, we know nothing from Acts or Paul's letters regarding the background of his Roman citizenship. We do know that this was undoubtedly an authentic claim. Lying about such matters resulted in dire consequences.

The commander stopped the preparations for scourging Paul, but he was still bewildered by the intense antagonism of the mob that had threatened him. The commander wanted to know why they were intent on killing him. Therefore, the next day the commander had Paul brought before the council of the Sanhedrin.

As Paul began to address the Sanhedrin, Ananias, the high priest, ordered that Paul be struck on the mouth. This act reminds us of a similar striking of Jesus (John 18:22). In language very much like that used by Jesus when he criticized the scribes and Pharisees (Matthew 23:27–28), Paul defiantly called Ananias a "white-washed wall" and a violator of the Jewish law. When Paul was reminded that he was disrespectfully addressing "God's high priest," he replied with biting sarcasm that he couldn't tell by Ananias' actions that he was the high priest.

Paul seemed to be in very deep trouble. But he apparently devised a cunning act, which disrupted the deliberations of the council. Realizing that the Sanhedrin was composed of both Pharisees and Sadducees, and that those two groups were often very antagonistic toward each other, Paul decided to capitalize on their differences in order to produce dissension between them. He claimed that he was a Pharisee himself and that the only reason he was on trial was that he was proclaiming the belief of the Pharisees that the dead would be raised. The Pharisees present immediately saw Paul in a more positive light, and when the Sadducees, who did not believe in the resurrection of the dead, began to argue with them over this point, chaos resulted. Afraid that Paul would be harmed in the scuffle, the Roman commander sent soldiers to rescue him.

The next night, while Paul was still in Roman custody, he had a vision in which he was assured that he would bear his testimony for Jesus in Rome. God was in control of history and God's will was to be accomplished in spite of the evil acts of human beings.

There is a recurring pattern in three of the main scenes in this section of Acts that may be of interest to us. In each of these scenes there are three common elements. (1) Paul was confronted by those who opposed his work (21:27–28; 21:40;

22:30). (2) In each instance the opposition threatened his life (21:31, 36; 22:22; 23:10). (3) The Roman authorities rescued Paul from dangerous circumstances (21:31–32; 22:30; 23:10). In this pattern we can begin to see Luke's understanding that the Roman government might have served as a protector of Christians when they were faced by violent crowds. Moreover, in Paul's appeal to his Roman citizenship we can perceive Luke's judgment that "Christians have [an] apostolic example [in Paul] to legitimate their use of their legal rights as a protection against injustice (see 16:37–39)."[1] While Luke did not consider the state to be without flaws, he was much more sympathetic to the role of the state than some later Christian writers. For example, the author of Revelation, who wrote at a time when the Roman empire was actively persecuting the church, projected a very negative view of the civil government.

Paul Sent to Caesarea (23:12—26:32)

While Paul was being held in the Roman barracks in Jerusalem, a plot was devised by his opponents to assassinate him. It was not the first time his murder had been planned (20:3). This time, Luke stated, more than forty persons took an oath not to eat or drink until Paul had been killed. They announced their plans to the leaders of the religious establishment and prepared to ambush Paul the next time he was brought to the council of the Sanhedrin.

The plot to kill Paul was thwarted, however, when his nephew overheard the plans for the ambush. He hurried to the barracks and told his uncle about the scheme to have him murdered. Paul then sent his nephew to tell the commander (tribune) what he had heard. The commander listened to the story and sent the young man off after pledging him to secrecy. The commander called two of his officers and ordered them to move Paul to Caesarea about nine o'clock that night. An unusually large guard of 470 men was to accompany the prisoner to guarantee his safe delivery to Caesarea. (Prisoners who were also Roman citizens received special attention.)

Claudius Lysias, the commander, sent a letter with the expedition in which he attempted to explain the circumstances surrounding Paul's trouble in Jerusalem and his claim to Roman citizenship. The letter was addressed to Felix, the

Roman procurator (governor) of Judea who ruled from about A.D. 52 to 59. The gist of the letter was that Paul had been accused of holding certain religious views contrary to the Jewish law. While the commander did not consider Paul's views deserving of imprisonment or death, Paul's opponents had plotted his assassination. He ended his letter by saying that he felt Felix could better deal with this case.

When the military escort arrived with Paul in Caesarea, they delivered him with the commander's letter to Felix. The procurator ordered Paul to be held in the former palace of Herod the Great until his accusers could travel to Caesarea to explain their charges against him.

After a short time Paul's antagonists from Jerusalem arrived in Caesarea and laid out their case against him. Through their representative, Tertullus, they charged him with stirring up trouble among the Jews in his extensive travels. They alleged that he was the key leader of the Nazarenes (another name given to the followers of Jesus), a messianic movement, which they stated was a threat to Roman rule. Finally, they claimed that Paul had desecrated the temple, the sanctity of which had been guaranteed by the Roman government. For this last offense they had seized him. Tertullus asserted that these accusations would prove true when Felix examined Paul for himself. All of this, of course, set the stage for a speech by Paul in which he was given the opportunity to answer the charges made against him.

The speech delivered by Paul made several key points. First, Paul denied that he was an agitator and that he had desecrated the temple. Second, although he was affiliated with the Way, which many understood to be a wayward and unorthodox form of Judaism, he considered himself a loyal Jew. He worshipped God and respected the law and the prophets. It was also his belief that there would be a resurrection in which the righteous would be rewarded and the unjust would be punished. Third, Paul claimed that he was diligent regarding his responsibility to God and other people. Fourth, he indicated that one of the principal reasons for his visit to Jerusalem was to bring to his sisters and brothers from their friends in the Gentile churches an offering for the poor. (See also Romans 15:25; I Corinthians 16:1–4). This was another demonstration of unity between Jewish and Gentile Christians. Furthermore, while Paul was engaged in this charitable work, he had gone to the temple for a purification ceremony (21:26). Paul, of course, was intimating that none of this sounded like the deeds of someone who disrespected the law and the temple, the two most revered institutions of Judaism. So far as he could determine, there was only one legitimate complaint, which some made against him. He did proclaim the resurrection of the dead. But so did the Pharisees!

Felix decided to defer any decision about Paul for two reasons. First, Luke stated that Felix knew enough about the Way that he was reluctant to treat Christians unjustly. Second, he wanted to hear more from Claudius Lysias, the commander, who knew the details about the attack on Paul in Jerusalem. Although Paul was kept in prison, he was permitted some freedom including visits from his friends.

On one of the days that followed, Felix and his wife Drusilla, who was Jewish, sent for Paul and invited him to speak with them about faith in Christ. Paul also used the occasion to address Felix regarding justice, self-control and the future judgment, three topics not only pertinent to faith in Christ, but also to the behavior of Felix who was known for his brutality. Felix was disturbed by Paul's plain-speaking about these matters and ended their conversation. He was also disappointed that Paul did not offer him a bribe for his release.

On other occasions over the next two years while Paul was in Felix' custody, he was summoned by the governor and they talked with each other. Although Felix may not have found enough fault in Paul to sentence him to any definite punishment or even to send him on to Rome, he also refused to release him since that would anger Paul's influential enemies. It seems that Felix was not as committed to justice as he was to doing what was politically expedient.

When Porcius Festus succeeded Felix as procurator of Judea, he was informed by the Jewish leaders in Jerusalem about the prisoner named Paul who had been left in confinement by Felix. They asked that Paul be released and brought to Jerusalem. They also planned to ambush and kill him on the way. Festus refused to have Paul delivered to Jerusalem. Instead, he requested that Paul's accusers travel to Caesarea to state their charges against him.

A few days later, after Festus had returned from Jerusalem to

Caesarea, Paul's adversaries appeared before the procurator and presented their charges. Paul denied their accusations and refused Festus' offer to release him for trial in Jerusalem. In a bold and dramatic speech Paul asserted that if he had done anything to deserve death, he should be so punished, but that he had committed no offense against either Judaism or Rome. In his closing remarks Paul appealed for a hearing before Caesar himself, the Roman emperor (25:11). According to Roman law at that time, every Roman citizen possessed the right of direct appeal to the emperor. After Festus consulted with his advisers, he announced that Paul would be sent to Rome for the hearing he had requested with Caesar.

Before Paul could be shipped from Caesarea to Rome he had a final confrontation with an important Jewish leader, King Herod Agrippa II. The king was the son of Herod Agrippa I whose death was described in Acts 12:23. Agrippa II had been declared king by the Romans and had been given control over territory in northeast Palestine. He also possessed the authority to appoint the high priest. Agrippa and Bernice, his sister, traveled to Caesarea to greet Festus, the new procurator. During their visit, Festus told Agrippa and Bernice the story of Paul's imprisonment and the attempt of his enemies to have him condemned. He explained that Paul had refused to be tried in Jerusalem and had appealed for a hearing before the emperor. Agrippa's curiosity was aroused. He wanted to hear Paul for himself.

The following day Festus, Agrippa, Bernice, and a group of important military officers and prominent citizens of Caesarea gathered in the governor's palace to hear Paul. In an opening statement, Festus expressed hope that as a result of the hearing Agrippa might help him clarify the charges against Paul, which he would have to send to the emperor with the prisoner. The stage was again set for a lengthy address by Paul in his own defense (26:2–23).

Paul's address began with the usual complimentary remarks, which were intended to secure a favorable hearing by those present (26:2–3; compare with 24:2–4). The remainder of the speech was in an autobiographical form similar to Paul's earlier speech before the angry mob in Jerusalem (22:3–21). Paul recalled his earlier life as a Pharisee and persecutor of Christians. He confessed that he had done everything possible to destroy the Christian movement in Jerusalem and everywhere else he could locate it. But God had changed him in an extraordinary experience on the road to Damascus. This was the third time in Acts that Paul's conversion was described (26:12–18; compare with 9:1–19 and 22:3–16), which underscored its importance in Luke's estimation. There are two differences between the description of the experience given at Caesarea and the earlier accounts of it. First, at Caesarea Paul made no mention of Ananias. Second, the speech at Caesarea contained a longer and more detailed account of Paul's commission to carry the Christian message to the Gentiles, "to open their eyes, that they may turn from darkness to light and from the power of Satan to God, that they may receive forgiveness of sins and a place among those who are sanctified by faith in [Christ]" (26:18).

In the final section of his speech at Caesarea (26:19–23) Paul stated that he had been totally obedient to the Lord's commission. He had declared in Damascus, in Jerusalem, throughout Judea, and to the Gentiles that people must repent and change their ways. He had said nothing contrary to the law or the prophets who had written that the Messiah (Christ) must suffer, be raised from the dead, and proclaim new life to all.

By the time Paul had completed his speech, Festus was convinced that he was a lunatic. Paul's study of all that business about God had driven him mad. Without losing his composure, however, Paul asserted that he had merely spoken the truth. He suspected that Agrippa understood his testimony. When he asked the king for a response, Agrippa answered evasively.

The outcome of Paul's appearance and interrogation was that Festus and Agrippa could find nothing in his words or deeds that deserved either imprisonment or death. Ironically, Agrippa stated that if Paul had not appealed to Caesar, he could have been set free. The hearing demonstrated that Christianity had emerged, "as a responsible and respectable religion, and Paul himself was guiltless of any offense against the imperial government."[2]

Voyage to Rome (27:1—28:15)

This section of Acts contains the story of Paul's voyage from Caesarea to Rome including the account of his being shipwrecked. It was written with the assumption that despite every difficulty and hazard, it was God's intention that Paul should proclaim the Christian message in Rome.

Paul was delivered to a centurion named Julius in whose custody he was to make the journey to Rome. Julius was described as someone who treated Paul with kindness and allowed him a certain degree of freedom on the voyage. Paul was accompanied by friends, one of whom, Aristarchus, was specifically named. Since the author again used the pronoun "we" in this section, it may be that he was also present on the voyage.

From Caesarea the ship that carried Paul stopped at Sidon and Myra. When it reached Fair Havens on the southern side of Crete, Paul warned the centurion Julius that since the fast (the Day of Atonement) had passed, it was not a safe season for sailing. Paul was afraid that the ship, its cargo and the lives of those on board would be lost if they continued to sail when the weather conditions were dangerous. The ship's captain and its owner assured the centurion, however, that they could sail safely to the nearby harbor of Phoenix where they would spend the winter. As the ship headed for Phoenix it was caught in a violent storm and driven out to sea. The crew undergirded the ship, probably by passing ropes under its hull and tying them together on the deck and by stretching cables from the bow to the stern to prevent the ship from breaking apart. They lowered gear, perhaps an anchor, to slow the ship. Finally, they began to jettison the cargo and any equipment that was expendable. There was little improvement in the weather or in the maneuverability of the ship. The crew and passengers abandoned any hope that they would survive.

In this desperate situation Paul reminded those on board that they should have heeded his warning about not leaving Fair Havens. But he also shared with them the news that God had assured him that while the ship would be lost, there would not be any loss of life. It was God's will that Paul would testify to his faith before Caesar. Therefore, his life would be spared as well as the lives of those who sailed with him.

The ship was adrift when some of the crew realized that they were nearing land. They let out anchors from the stern to insure that if the ship went aground it would do so with the bow facing the land. Some of the sailors tried to escape by a small boat, but Paul warned that they must be kept on board since everyone's help would be needed to get the crew and passengers safely to shore.

As day began to dawn, Paul urged his shipmates to eat in order to give them sufficient strength for the final episode of their ordeal. Again he assured them that no one would be harmed. In an exemplary fashion Paul himself took some bread, gave thanks to God, and began to eat it. Though this act resembles somewhat a celebration of the Lord's Supper, it appears to be more along the lines of an ordinary meal. After those on board had eaten—276 persons according to Luke— they further lightened the ship by throwing its wheat cargo into the sea.

When daylight finally came, the crew realized that they could run the ship aground on the beach of the bay in which they were located. The anchors were cut loose, the rudders were freed and the small foresail was raised to maneuver the ship toward the beach. Before the ship reached the beach it struck a shoal. The bow stuck fast, but the raging surf began to break up the stern of the ship. At that moment there was a crisis. Since the soldiers were responsible for their prisoners and would be held accountable if any of them escaped (remember the Philippian jailer's fear about this in 16:25–27), the soldiers were prepared to kill their captives. The centurion, Julius, intervened in order to save Paul and ordered everyone to swim, or to float with pieces of the wrecked ship, toward land. Luke reported that Paul's prediction came true. Everyone was able to make it safely to shore.

Only after the crew and passengers were on land did they learn that they were on Malta, an island about sixty miles south of Sicily. Luke stated that Paul and his companions resided on the island for the next three months until it was safe to sail again. While they were on Malta, Luke reported two incidents in which Paul was the central figure.

The first incident occurred shortly after the ship's party had escaped to shore (28:2–6). The natives of the island treated them with great kindness. They greeted them warmly and built a fire to make them comfortable. As Paul helped to gather wood for the fire, a poisonous snake bit him on the hand. When the natives saw what had happened they concluded that Paul was guilty of a most serious crime. In the ancient world it was commonly believed that divine forces in nature and the animal world punished wickedness. Maybe Paul had escaped drowning, but surely now he would pay for the evil deeds of which he must be guilty. The natives waited for Paul to collapse and die from the viper's bite. But he did not die. He showed no ill effects at all. Instead of thinking Paul an evil person, therefore, the natives proclaimed that he was a god. His survival meant to them that he was not only innocent, but also more than a human being. That natives considered Paul a god recalls the incident at Lystra where Paul and Barnabas were thought to be divine and given the names of the Greek gods Hermes and Zeus (14:8–18). The point of this story for Luke seems clear. Nature confirmed what the authorities had ascertained at Caesarea, namely, that Paul was a righteous man.

The second incident on Malta concerned a man named Publius, the Roman governor of the island. According to Luke, Publius was especially kind to Paul. When Publius' father became sick, Paul visited him, prayed for him, and laid hands on him. As a result he was miraculously healed. Subsequently, the news about the healing spread and others around the island came to Paul and were healed of their diseases. Near the end of Acts, therefore, we find another illustration of the church's concern for the physical well-being of people.

When the weather was favorable for continuing their journey, Paul and his companions were presented gifts from the inhabitants of Malta and they set sail for Italy. Stops were made at the ports of Syracuse, Rhegium and Puteoli. At Puteoli Paul discovered some Christians who were hospitable to him. After several days there, the group traveled on to Rome. On the way, at the Forum of Appius and at Three Taverns, they were met by Christians who had come from Rome to greet them. Paul was grateful to know that there were sisters and brothers in Christ nearby who could encourage and comfort him. When he arrived in Rome, Paul was permitted to stay in his own private quarters with only one soldier to guard him.

Paul in Rome (28:17–31)

After Paul had been in Rome for three days he invited the leaders of the local Jewish synagogue to meet with him. He wanted to inform them about the circumstances that led to his being in Rome. When they had gathered, Paul stated to them that although he had been loyal to the Jewish people and their traditions, he had been charged with preaching against Judaism. He had been arrested and sent from Jerusalem to Rome as a prisoner. The authorities who examined him in Caesarea could find no reason why he should not be released. However, when his opponents objected to his being set free, he was forced to appeal his case to Caesar since he was a Roman citizen. Furthermore, he did not wish to bring a countercharge against his people. He ended his address by implying that he was nothing but a loyal Jew whose concern for "the hope of Israel" had gotten him into deep trouble. At this point, Luke did not record whether Paul explained that his concept of "the hope of Israel" included the declaration of Jesus as the Christ (Messiah) and belief in the resurrection of the dead.

The response of the assembled Jewish leaders was that they had not heard anything negative about Paul either by letter or through other reports by visitors to Rome. They did know something about the Christian "sect," however, and that it was generally criticized. Nevertheless, they wanted to hear more from Paul. A date was set for another meeting wtih him.

Paul's second meeting with the Jewish leaders was held in the place where he was living. He spent virtually a whole day speaking to them about the kingdom of God and trying to convince them that Jesus was the Christ, the Messiah, the Anointed One of God. These were among the most important themes in the preaching and teaching of the early church according to Luke (see, for example, Acts 8:12 and 28:31). Paul received the same mixed response to his ideas here as he had experienced elsewhere in his travels. Some were convinced by what he said. Others were not.

As the group left Paul's residence they argued among themselves, but not before Paul made a final statement to them. Quoting Isaiah 6:1–10 (see also Luke 8:10), he sadly observed that what the Holy Spirit had spoken through the prophet to their ancestors was true of many of them also. They heard, but did not understand. They saw, but never really noticed. They had grown dull. Their hearing, seeing and understanding had been impaired to the point that they were unable to turn to God to be healed and made whole. Therefore, God had directed the message of saving power to be proclaimed to the Gentiles (see Psalm 67:2).

Luke concluded his book by saying that Paul remained in Rome for two more years, possibly engaged in some sort of work that brought him an income. Working in this way was not unusual for prisoners awaiting their trials. During this period he cordially received visitors and without interference he openly preached about the kingdom of God and Jesus the Christ. So, as William Neil comments,

> The commission of the risen Christ to his first disciples to be his witnesses from Jerusalem to the end of the earth (1:8) [had] been fulfilled in the richest measure by the greatest of all the apostles. The Gospel [had] been firmly planted in the capital of the Empire, and with the intimation that it was being proclaimed there by Paul quite openly and unhindered, Luke brings his masterly account of the first three decades of the history of the church to a perfect dramatic conclusion . . . .[3]

There is one matter of unfinished business, of course. Luke never reported on Paul's fate. What happened to him? At least three suggestions have been made. Some believe that Paul was simply released by the emperor before any trial took place. Others hold that he was tried and declared innocent of the charges made against him. Most, however, feel that Paul was probably martyred in Rome about A.D. 62. His martyrdom at Rome seems well attested in the tradition of the early church.

Acts for Our Time

In this chapter we have dealt with the final episodes of Luke's story of the early church. They center almost exclusively on the last years of Paul's work. They trace his steps from Jerusalem to Caesarea and then on to Rome. As in the other parts of Acts, there are a number of issues that these sections may raise for us.

One of the more important questions raised by this part of Acts has to do with its understanding of the role of the state. We noted earlier that Luke made it clear that the Roman government generally served as a protector of Christians when they were threatened with violence by their opponents. Paul was rescued by the Roman commander (tribune) in Jerusalem when the mob planned to kill him (21:31–36; 22:22–24a). The Roman officials, Felix and Festus, refused to release Paul to be tried by his opposition in Jerusalem, thereby undoubtedly saving his life. Luke, however, did show that the state's role was not without fault. The tribune intended to have Paul scourged in Jerusalem. Felix desired a bribe from Paul and when he did not get it, he held Paul in prison as a favor to his antagonists. Nevertheless, Luke usually portrayed the state as a defender of Christians. Even in Ephesus Paul was saved by the intervention of the town clerk (19:35–41). Luke tried to demonstrate throughout Acts that the early Christian community was not seeking the violent overthrow of the state. The early Christians were simply obedient, law-abiding citizens, one of the emphases Paul made in his speeches (24:16) and a major point in the judgment about Paul by Festus and Agrippa (26:31).

The view of the state in Acts is considerably different from that which we discover in Daniel where civil disobedience against the state is sometimes required (see Daniel 3 and 6), or in Revelation where the Roman state was pictured as an evil beast and a wicked harlot (Revelation 13 and 17) that demanded idolatrous practices from God's people and threatened them with violence if they did not comply. There is an obvious tension between the relationship of God's people and the state, as portrayed in Acts, and that portrayed in the books of Daniel and Revelation. That same tension may be reflected in our relationship with the state today. On the one hand, the state may be viewed positively as the institution that guarantees freedom of religion. It may protect our right to worship and to practice our religious beliefs according to our consciences. In the United States that right is guaranteed by the nation's Constitution. The federal government is charged with insuring the Constitution's mandate of religious freedom. On the other hand, the state may be engaged in acts that Christians think of as contrary to God's will. Consequently, Christians may find themselves involved in protests and acts of civil disobedience against what they consider to be the misuse of power by the state. From the first decades of the church's history to the present, Christians have often found themselves living in this sort of tension.

A second issue raised in this section as well as throughout Acts is the conviction that the church's mission cannot and will not succeed unless God empowers, guides and directs it. From the time he arrived in Jerusalem through his appearances before the hostile crowds and civil authorities, and through his

99

nearly tragic shipwreck until his final preaching in Rome, Paul was pictured by Luke as a person who was invested with power and led by the Spirit. His achievements were not the result of clever deception or shrewd marketing. They were produced by opening up his life to be filled with the Holy Spirit and the gifts that accompanied the Spirit. One of the most important lessons we can learn from Acts is that God invites us to ministry and mission and offers us the presence and power of the Spirit as we faithfully pursue God's plan for the world in which we live.

Furthermore, as Jacques Dupont reminds us,

> The upheaval that the first generation of Christians lived through cannot but interest Christians of today who have the impression that everything, both in our world and in our Church, is undergoing change. The history which the Acts of the Apostles narrates provides us with a model that we can imitate, because it teaches us what form fidelity to Jesus and his Gospel must take in times of change. Acts does not encourage fruitless clinging to a past which may have been very beautiful in its time but which is really gone. It does inspire in us a concern to live the spirit of Jesus and his message in a present which is always new, and a conviction that the same Spirit Jesus sent upon his apostles continues to be active in the Church of our day.[4]

Questions and Suggestions

1. Why did Luke devote so much space in Acts to the story of Paul's arrest, the hearings before governmental officials, and his voyage to Rome?

2. What do you think is the proper relationship between the church and the state? Do you ever feel any tension between your commitment to the faith and your loyalty to the nation?

3. We have read about a large number of personalities in Acts. With which one of them are you most able to identify? Is there any way in which you feel that the story of that person is like your own?

4. Now that you have read through, thought about, and discussed Acts, why do you think Luke wrote it? What was his purpose?

5. As a group, discuss how this study of Acts has changed your minds on any issue or how it has confirmed your views

about Christian faith and life. If you wrote a definition of the church and a description of its mission, as was suggested in the first session, perhaps you could reexamine those statements now, and revise them as you feel necessary, having completed the study.

6. What do you intend to do as a result of this study of Acts? What actions are appropriate as a response to the presence and power of the Holy Spirit, which we have encountered through our reading, study and fellowship?

7. A carefully planned worship period would be appropriate to end this study, with hymns, scripture readings and prayers that would focus on the Holy Spirit, our commission to be Christ's witnesses, and the needs of the world in which we live.

NOTES

Chapter I

1. William Neil, *The Acts of the Apostles*, New Century Bible Commentary. (Grand Rapids, Michigan: William B. Eerdmans, 1981), p. 27.
2. H. J. Cadbury, "Acts of the Apostles," *The Interpreter's Dictionary of the Bible* (Nashville, Abingdon Press, 1962), I, p. 34.
3. Leonard Swidler, *Biblical Affirmations of Woman* (Philadelphia: The Westminster Press, 1979), p. 294.

Chapter II

1. Neil, p. 66.
2. I. Howard Marshall, *The Acts of the Apostles: An Introduction and Commentary* (Grand Rapids, Michigan: William B. Eerdmans, 1980), p. 64.
3. Halford E. Luccock, *Marching Off the Map* (New York: Harper and Brothers, 1952), p. 144.
4. Prayer by Eric Milner-White and G. W. Briggs, George Appleton, editor, *The Oxford Book of Prayer* (New York: Oxford University Press, 1985), p. 155.

Chapter III

1. Neil, p. 84.
2. Charles H. Talbert, *Acts*, John Knox Preaching Guides (Atlanta: John Knox Press, 1984), p. 22.
3. Talbert, p. 24.
4. Talbert, p. 28.

Chapter IV

1. Talbert, p. 31.
2. Talbert, p. 34.
3. Talbert, p. 38.
4. Quoted in Helmut Gollwitzer, Kathe Kuhn and Reinhold Schneider, editors, *Dying We Live* (New York: The Seabury Press, 1956), p. 203.

Chapter V

1. Talbert, p. 70.
2. Martin Luther King, Jr., *Why We Can't Wait* (New York: New American Library, 1964), p. 91.

Chapter VI

1. Talbert, p. 95.
2. Neil, p. 246.
3. Neil, p. 259.
4. Jacques Dupont, *The Salvation of the Gentiles: Studies in the Acts of the Apostles* (New York: Paulist Press, 1979), pp. 9-10.

RESOURCES FOR FURTHER STUDY

For those who are interested in exploring additional resources in their study of the Acts of the Apostles, there are a number of places where excellent material can be found.

Valuable reference help will be found in the recently published *Harper's Bible Dictionary*, edited by Paul J. Achtemeier (San Francisco: Harper and Row, 1985) and in *The Interpreter's Dictionary of the Bible*, edited by George A. Buttrick and Keith Crim (Nashville: Abingdon Press, 1962 and 1976). Both of these reference works contain a large number of excellent articles on topics, places, persons and concepts found in Acts.

A variety of outstanding commentaries are also available to assist us in our study of the book. Laypeople will find the following especially useful: Robert J. Karris, *Invitation to Acts: A Commentary on the Acts of the Apostles with Complete Text from the Jerusalem Bible* (New York: Image Books, 1978); I. Howard Marshall, *The Acts of the Apostles: An Introduction and Commentary* (Grand Rapids, Michigan: William B. Eerdmans, 1980); and William Neil, *The Acts of the Apostles* (Grand Rapids, Michigan: William B. Eerdmans, 1981).

For any who want additional resources on a more advanced level, the following are recommended: Ernst Haenchen, *The Acts of the Apostles: A Commentary* (Philadelphia: The Westminster Press, 1971); Johannes Munck, *The Acts of the Apostles* (Garden City, New York, 1967); and Charles H. Talbert, *Acts* (Atlanta: John Knox Press, 1984).

Works that would be helpful to those interested in the role of women in the New Testament church might include: *In Memory of Her* by Elisabeth Schüssler Fiorenza, Crossroad Press, 1985; *Women and Ministry in the New Testament* by Elisabeth M. Tetlow, University Press of America, 1985 and Leonard Swidler's *Biblical Affirmations of Woman*, Westminster Press, 1979. You might check the index of each book, note the references to the book of Acts, read these passages, get the author's point of view, then discuss the issues.